# Get Your Book *Published*

Barbara A. Fanson

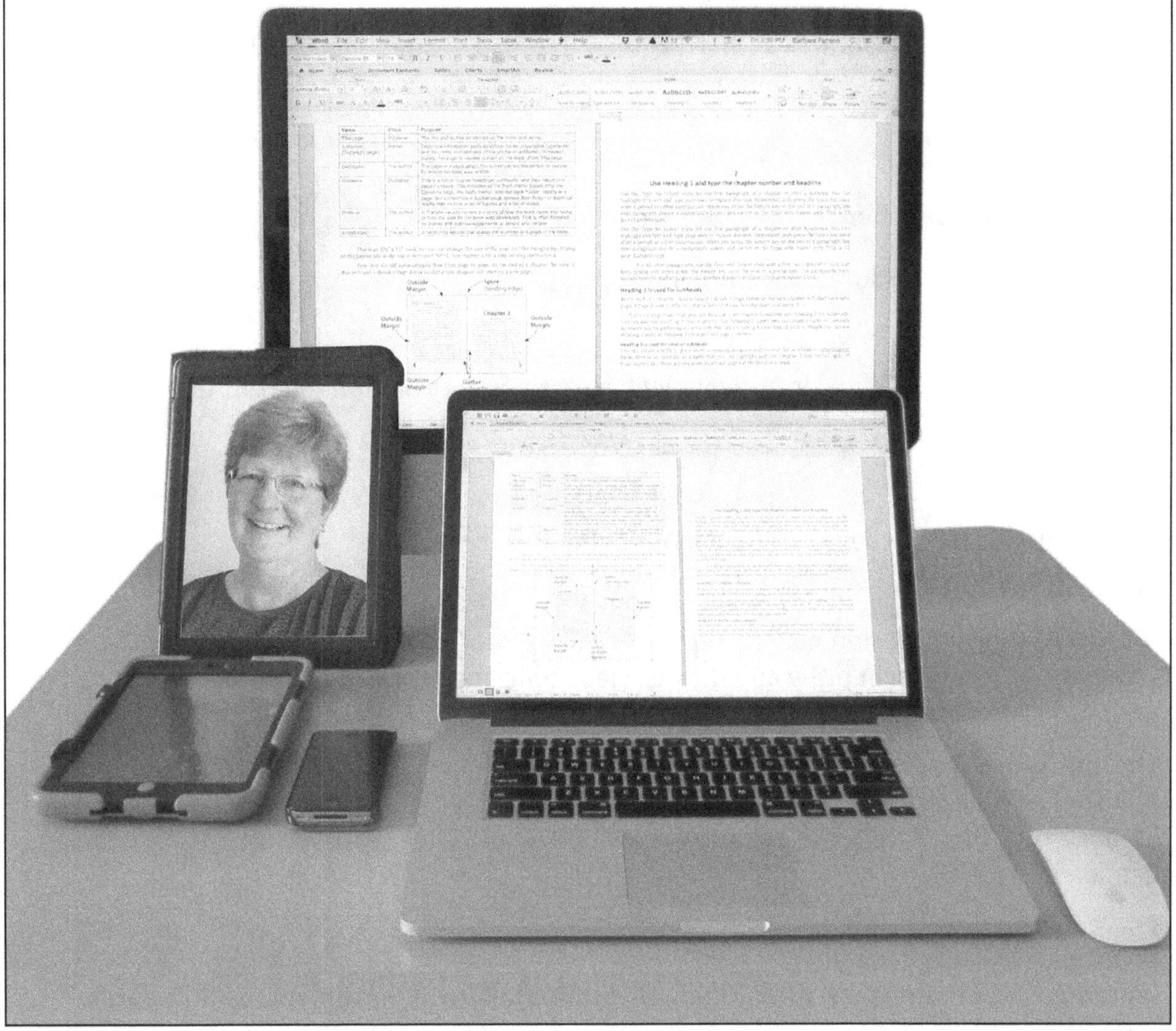

Dedicated to my personal consultant Kristen Van Kampen.

Author and graphic designer Barbara A. Fanson wrote *Robin Sees a Monster* and *Shirl the Squirrel Rises to New Heights*, children's picture books and *Tragedy on the Twenty*, a historical fiction book. She has also written over 30 non-fiction books including *Milestones & Memories, Preserving Smithville, Illustrator One Step at a Time, Start & Run a Desktop Publishing Business,* and *Producing a First-Class Newsletter.*

She lives in Hamilton, Ontario with a dashing black cat, 7 squirrels, 2 robins, a rabbit, and her human family.

**Get Your Book Published**

Published by Sterling Education Centre Inc.
http://fanson.net

Thank you for reading. If you have a moment, please post a review on Amazon, Goodreads or Kirkus Reviews. Thank you.

Copyright © 2019 Barbara A. Fanson. All Rights Reserved.
Book ISBN: 978-1-989361-11-5

No part of this publication may be reproduced or stored in a retrieval system, or transmitted in any form or by any means, electronic, mechanical, recording, or otherwise, without written permission of the publisher:

Sterling Education Centre Inc.
220 Homebrook Drive
Mount Hope, ON
Canada L0R 1W0

Email: Barbara@Fanson.net

IngramSpark, CreateSpace, KDP, Kindle Direct Publishing, Amazon, Adobe Illustrator, Adobe Photoshop, and any other names are trademarks of their perspective companies.

# Table of Contents

Preface ................................................................................................................ v
1 Three ways to get your book published ........................................................ 1
   Steps to publishing a print book online .................................................... 2
   Comparison of earnings for a book priced at $24.99 ................................ 3
   Comparison of earnings for a book priced at $15 ..................................... 4
2 Writing the story ............................................................................................ 8
   Proofing your story ..................................................................................... 8
   Formatting your story ................................................................................. 8
   Traditional printing versus print on demand ............................................. 9
3 Traditional book publishing .......................................................................... 11
   Research existing books ............................................................................ 11
   Check the publisher's website .................................................................. 12
   Write a query letter .................................................................................. 12
4 Self-Publishing a book .................................................................................. 14
   Hybrid Publishing ...................................................................................... 14
   Vanity Publishers ....................................................................................... 14
   Publish a book yourself ............................................................................. 15
   Different styles of books ........................................................................... 16
   Different types of books ........................................................................... 18
5 Do you need illustrations or photographs? .................................................. 20
   Add Alt Text to images .............................................................................. 20
   What file format should you use for images? .......................................... 22
6 Should the book have a bleed or no bleed? ................................................. 23
7 Designing a book cover ................................................................................ 25
   Designing the back cover .......................................................................... 26
   Can you have type on the spine? .............................................................. 28
   Extra artwork for case bound or hardcover books ................................... 30
   Add a dust jacket ...................................................................................... 30
8 Book Trim Size .............................................................................................. 32
   Comparison of three printers ................................................................... 35
   Where can you get good quality images? ................................................ 37
   Vector Graphics versus Raster Graphics .................................................. 37

| | |
|---|---|
| **9 Prepare your book for upload** | 38 |
| Add an ISBN and Barcode to Your Book | 39 |
| Designing a Cover | 41 |
| IngramSpark's Cover Generator | 42 |
| Working with the Cover Template | 45 |
| **10 Designing the front matter** | 53 |
| Front matter pages and their purpose | 54 |
| Designing the layout of a book | 56 |
| Headers and Footers | 61 |
| **11 Preparing a book for print** | 64 |
| Saving your book as a PDF | 64 |
| Book Checklist for Covers | 65 |
| Book Checklist for Interior Pages | 66 |
| What's the "key" to keywords? | 67 |
| Advantages to publishing with IngramSpark | 68 |
| Advantages to publishing with Amazon KDP | 68 |
| Uploading your book to IngramSpark | 69 |
| Converting currency for book prices | 77 |
| Uploading your book to Amazon | 79 |
| **About the Author** | 88 |
| **Book Publishing Terms** | 89 |

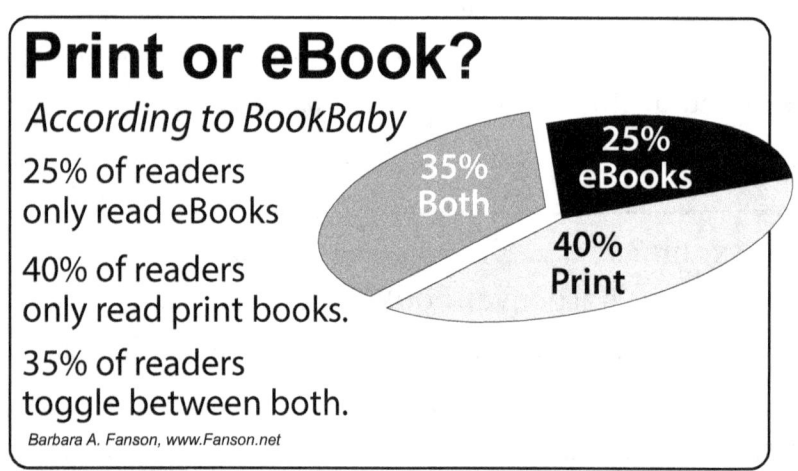

# Preface

"Desktop publishing will never catch on," my boss replied when I asked if the company would pay for my evening classes in Aldus PageMaker. They paid for classes in paste-up or film stripping, but they wouldn't pay for computer classes.

By 1990, that print shop went under and I was teaching desktop publishing classes at Seneca College to my fellow employees.

The graphics field has evolved beyond print, presentations, web design, social media, and book publishing.

What is the definition of a book?

Noun.

1. A written or printed work consisting of pages glued or sewn together along one side and bound in covers.
   "A book of selected poems"
2. A bound set of blank sheets for writing or keeping records in.
   "An accounts book."

I am a graphic designer who enjoys writing. I was the editor of my college newspaper, college professor, and an entrepreneur.

Which brings me to this book. *Get Your Book Published* shares much of the information I learned over the years printing and selling my books. The focus of this book is the actual printing and distribution of your book. We skim through writing, editing, and promoting your book so we focus on the publishing aspects of your book.

The four Ps of marketing are product, place, price, and promotion. This book deals with the first three. What **product** are you creating and how is yours different than others? What **places** will you sell or distribute your book: online, bookstores, schools, libraries, vendor events, festivals, or conferences? Price includes the cost to make it, sell it, and ship it. How will you **promote** your book is covered in my next book.

Today, there are many ways to get your story in front of readers.

30 years ago, traditional publishing was the only way to get your story published. I sent an inquiry letter to a publisher that specialized in how-to

instructional books with a table of contents and one chapter. They sent a contract to publish my book, pay me 10% of book sales, sell me copies of my book at 40% off so I could sell some at events, and the first right-of-refusal on my next two books. (If I write two more books, I have to show them the outline first, and if they choose not to publish them, I can approach another publisher.) *Producing a First-Class Newsletter* was born. Then I wrote *Start & Run a Desktop Publishing Business* and they published it.

I researched my family tree, organized a family reunion, and sold 100 books. I paid $11 to get *The Fanson Families of North America* photocopied and bound with plastic combs and sold them for $25. That was the first book that I wrote, designed, printed, and sold it myself. The year was 1990.

I was teaching computer software programs at the community college, so I wanted to publish my instructional books. The publishing company did not want to publish software books because they need updated often. I sold my books to students in the college's bookstore. I had the books photocopied and bound with plastic combs. I could update and add pages as necessary. Students could stand the book up and lean it against their computer. And then I marketed the books to other colleges. I did not realize in 1990 that I was self-publishing. The term wasn't popular yet. I have sold over 15,000 books in 30 titles including *Adobe Illustrator: One Step at a Time*.

Another college paid me a one-time fee of $800 for each software manual I wrote so they could photocopy and supply them to their students.

A local print shop wanted to specialize in newsletters, so I wrote and designed *The Newsletter Planning Guide*, which was a binder with pages. They wanted to add tabbed index pages and die-cutting to demonstrate their printing and bindery skills. In exchange for writing and designing the book, I was given 300 copies to sell or giveaway.

In 2015, I wrote and published a historical fiction book called *Tragedy on the Twenty*. Since it has local appeal, I visited almost every library within 50 km and a few historical societies. The print books or eBooks are available on Amazon and my website: Fanson.net.

*Milestones and Memories* is a baby record book and beyond. It took 15 years to perfect the book after having my first child. We share a joy of attending book festivals and author visits.

I wrote and illustrated *Shirl the Squirrel Rises to New Heights* because I enjoyed watching squirrels forge for food, protect themselves from predators, and realized they have different personalities.

*Robin Sees a Monster* combines my love of photography and nature. I have photographed birds and nature for years. I added two predators to the photographic album, which shows nest building, egg hatching, and fledglings learning to fly. The story is based on a real-life adventure.

In later chapters, I show you how to upload a Microsoft Word document or PDF file to Amazon and IngramSpark. Both charge a per book rate for printing a book; there are no quantity discounts. Whether you print 1 book or 5,000 books, the cost per book is the same.

If you're a beginner, I recommend uploading to Amazon first because it is easier and doesn't require as much information, but I have more sales with IngramSpark.

Booksellers and libraries usually buy their books from IngramSpark, so you'll want to upload a copy to their site, too. But, their website requires more Thema information for stores and libraries to categorize the book properly.

If you are planning to upload to both online book printers, do not turn on Global Distribution for Amazon; IngramSpark will provide global distribution. (Otherwise there could be a conflict with your ISBN.)

Some book printers like Tellwell Publishing use IngramSpark because they distribute lists of books to over 30,000 booksellers and libraries to see.

*Barbara A. Fanson*

# 1
# Three ways to get your book published

This chart compares the steps you would take from writing your story to seeing it published. You can assist with marketing your books, though the publisher will also do that. If you self-publish a book, you will have to do a lot more work and learn many more skills.

| Traditional Publisher | eBook | Self-Publishing |
|---|---|---|
| Write a story | Write a story | Write a story |
| Rewrite story | Rewrite story | Rewrite story |
| Send a query letter to a publisher | Edit story | Edit story |
| Make revisions as requested by editor | Format story | Format story |
| | Illustrations, photographs | Illustrations, photographs |
| | Design front cover | Design front cover |
| | Design interior pages | Design interior pages |
| | Proofread story | Proofread story |
| | Prepare description | Prepare description |
| | Create metadata | Create metadata |
| | Establish classifications | Establish classifications |
| | Market book | Supervise printing book |
| | Create a website | Market book |
| | Manage social media | Create a website |
| | Manage book sales | Manage social media |
| | Advertise to libraries, schools | Manage book sales |
| | | Advertise to libraries, schools |
| | | Ship books |
| | | Distribute to stores |

Barbara A. Fanson

# Steps to publishing a print book online

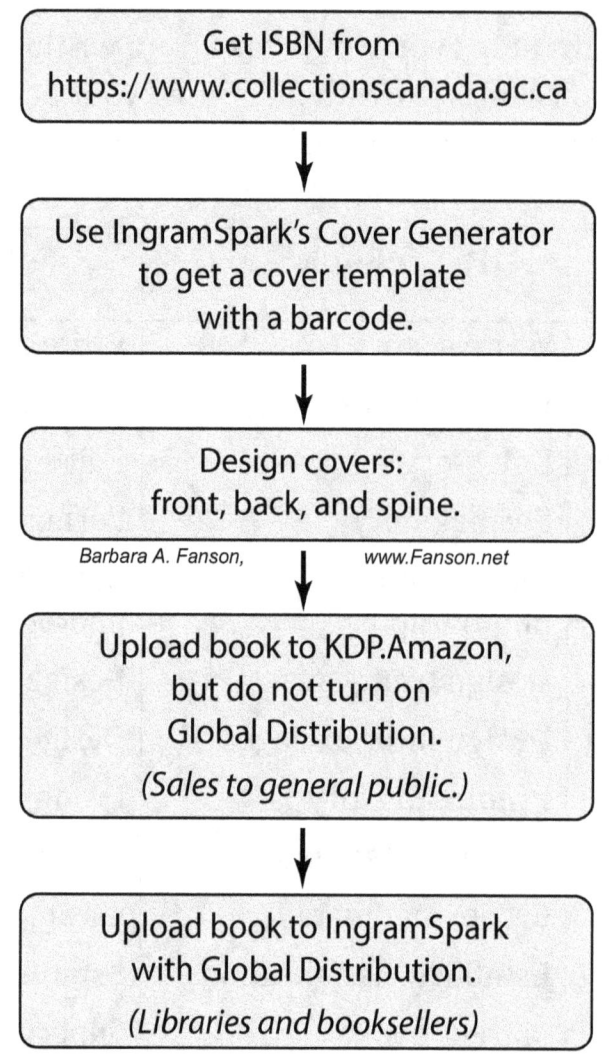

# Comparison of earnings for a book priced at $24.99

## Traditional book publisher:

A traditional book publisher may pay you 5 – 10% of sales. Assuming you have a publishing agreement of 10% or $2.49 per book sale. Every time a book is sold, the writer makes $2.49. Sell 100 books and you receive $249.
If it's a picture book, the author and illustrator may split 10%, so each person gets 5% or $1.25.

## Self-published book:

Booksellers and stores can buy the book for a discount of 40 – 55% off so they can resell it and make money.

$24.99 less 55% or $13.74 is $11.25. Booksellers can buy the book for $11.25 and resell for the regular price of $24.99 to pay for staff, store rent, and other expenses.

The self-publisher also has to pay for the printing of the book. The cost of printing depends on how many pages and whether it has color interior pages or black and white. Let's assume the printing of each book is $3.90.
$24.99 - $13.74 = $11.25 – $3.90 for printing = $7.35
You receive $7.35 per book or 29% to cover all your publishing and promotional expenses.

| Service Level Options: | ◉ Economy Service - Usually prints in 5 business days - $ 282.00 ○ Express Service - Usually prints in 2 business days - $ 309.00 ○ Rush Service - Usually prints in 1 business day - $ 363.00 |
|---|---|
| Shipping Options: | ◉ Canada Ground - $ 60.69 ○ Intl Economy(not trackable/insurable) - $ 169.53 ○ International Premium (including Canada) - $ 329.01 |

*Available Shipping Methods vary by print location.

| Ordered Qty | Book Type | Page Count | Service Level | Unit Selling Price | Extended Amount |
|---|---|---|---|---|---|
| 100 | Standard Color 8.5 x 11 in or 280 x 216 mm Perfect Bound on White w/Matte Lam | 40 | Usually prints in 5 business days. | $ 2.82 | $ 282.00 |
| | | | | Handling Fee | $ 4.99 |
| | | | | Subtotal | $ 286.99 |
| | | | | Shipping | $ 60.69 |
| | | | | Tax | $ 42.38 |
| | | | | Total | $ 390.06 |

# Comparison of earnings for a book priced at $15

**Traditional book publisher:**
A traditional book publisher may pay you 10% or $1.50 per book sale. Every time a book is sold, the writer makes $1.50. Sell 100 books and you receive $150.
If it's a picture book, the author and illustrator split the 10%, so each person gets 5% or $0.75.

**Self-published book:**
Booksellers and stores can buy the book for a discount of 55% off so they can resell it and make money. (40% discount too.)

$15 less 55% or $8.25 is $6.75. Booksellers can buy the book for $6.75 and resell for the regular price of $15 to pay for staff, store rent, and other expenses.

The self-publisher also has to pay for the printing of the book. The cost of printing depends on how many pages and whether it has color interior pages or black and white. Let's assume the printing each book is $3.90.

$15 - $8.25 = $6.75 – $3.90 for printing = $2.85

You receive $2.85 per book or 19% to cover all your publishing and promotional expenses.

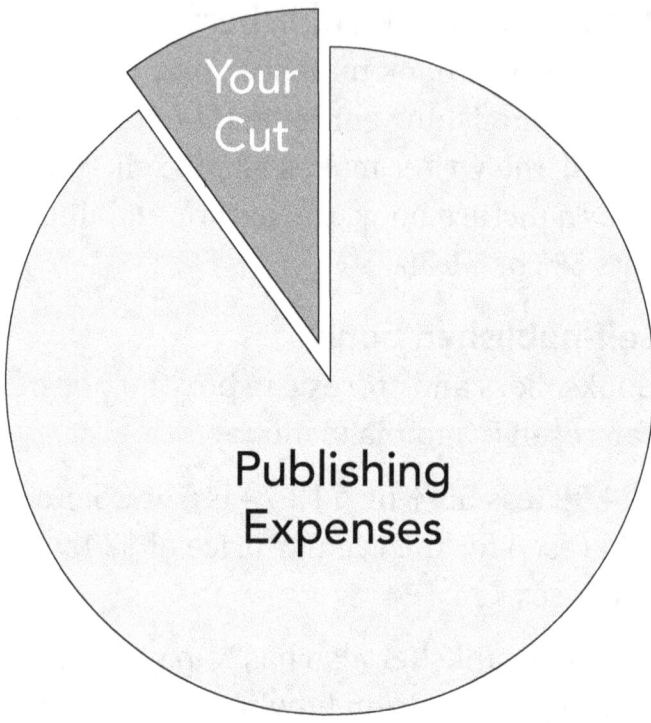

Figure 1: Traditionally-Published Book

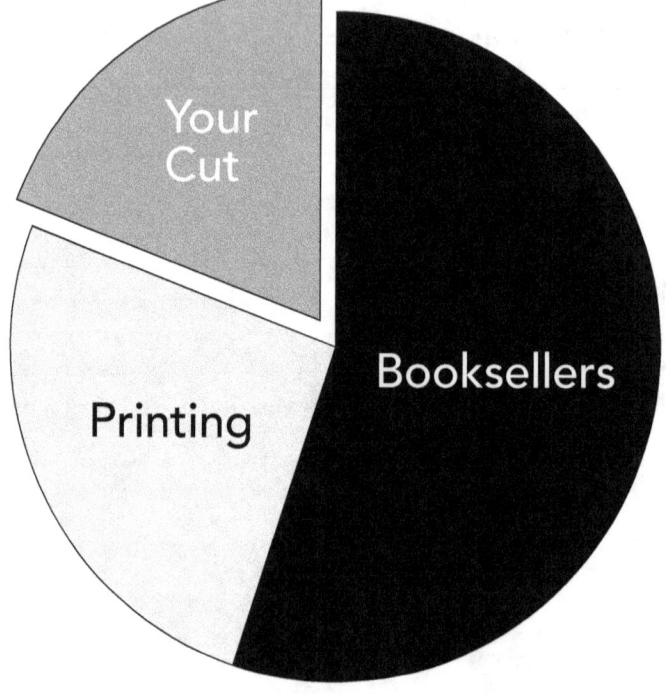

Figure 2: Self-Published Book

Or, 19% or $2.85 if you publish the book yourself. You have to pay for llustration, market, distribute, Internet, and a website to take orders.

If you're lucky, you can get your book into smaller, independent booksellers for 40% instead of 55%.

If you can sell copies of the book yourself, you get to keep that portion of 55%.

**Would you buy this book?**

As a self-publisher, you have to create a front cover yourself or hire someone. The cost of the artwork comes out of your cut. A traditional publisher would pay an artist to design a professional front cover for you.

As a self-publisher, you're responsible for designing the front cover, editing the interior pages and proofreading it. Will you hire someone or do it yourself? You're responsible for the cost.

Would you buy this book? It does not look like it was professionally designed, but you can buy it.

How will the books be sold? Will you design a commercial website to take book orders or hire someone? Again, you're responsible for the cost.

Will your book be sold in stores? How will you promote the book to booksellers? Or, will you pay a distributor?

Will you advertise on Facebook and other social media platforms? Can you design effective social media posts or hire someone?

The 19% of your cut that remained after paying for a booksellers discount and printing must be used to pay any additional expenses of publishing the book.

**Sell the book yourself**

If you choose to sell the books yourself by having a table at trade shows or going to independent booksellers, you will purchase copies of your book and pay for printing. If you get a museum or bookseller to stock your book, they may ask for 40% commission or consignment. Consignment is when you have books in a store but you don't get paid until the book sells. Normally, large booksellers buy books and resell them, but if you're an unknown author, stores may prefer consignment agreements.

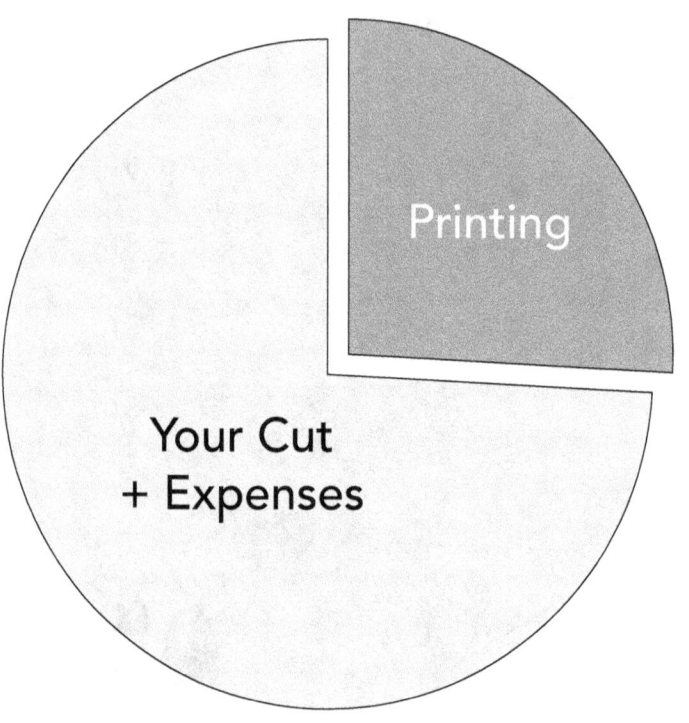

If you have a table at a trade show—like a knitter might have a table to sell their homemade items in a craft show—you will be one table of many so you're competing for the consumer's money and you'll want to promote the event to get more attendees.

I also purchase extra books for author events at libraries, schools, and special events. If you use a service like IngramSpark or Amazon, you pay for each book. You can buy 10 books or 15 books. You don't need to buy 1,000 books that require storage and then try to sell them. You may not sell any books at an author event.

If you're planning a family reunion, you may sell a few genealogical books to attendees. You could also organize a business event or seminar with books included in the admission price or sold at the end of the event.

Some people just print 5 or 10 books for themselves and sell the rest on Amazon or IngramSpark. You're relying on good marketing skills to make people aware of your books and direct them to the online sellers.

## What does the average children's book look like?

**Trim Size:** 8.5" x 8.5"

**Binding:** Hard Cover (Case Laminate)

**Laminate:** Gloss

**Paper:** 70lb. White

**Interior Color:** Standard Color

**Page Count:** 25

**List Price:** $22

**Retail Discount:** 53%

**Print Fee:** $6.94

**Compensation:** $3.40

*According to IngramSpark, these are the most common specifications for children's books.*

# 2
# Writing the story

You can write your story in Microsoft Word, Pages, InDesign, or Google Docs. Initially, just let the words flow. Don't worry about editing or formatting, just get the story out of your head and onto a page. Can you write better on a sheet of paper or do you prefer to type it into a computer or tablet? What is the best time of day for you to write?

## Proofing your story

The second step to getting your book published is to write a polished manuscript or story. It doesn't matter whether you get a publisher to produce it or you self-publish the book, the manuscript needs to be error-free. Please write and rewrite.

1. Use the spelling and grammar check in your software program to catch many errors.
2. Use a program like Grammarly.com to spot even more.
3. Now read your story out loud. Pretend you're reading to someone. Does it sound okay?
4. Print out your story on paper and read it again.
5. Have a friend who is pretty good with spelling and grammar read it. Maybe they can provide the first review. (IngramSpark asks for reviews.)
6. Once you're sure your story is polished, hire an editor. They are checking for more than just spelling. They will be looking at grammar, style, consistency, and formatting, too.

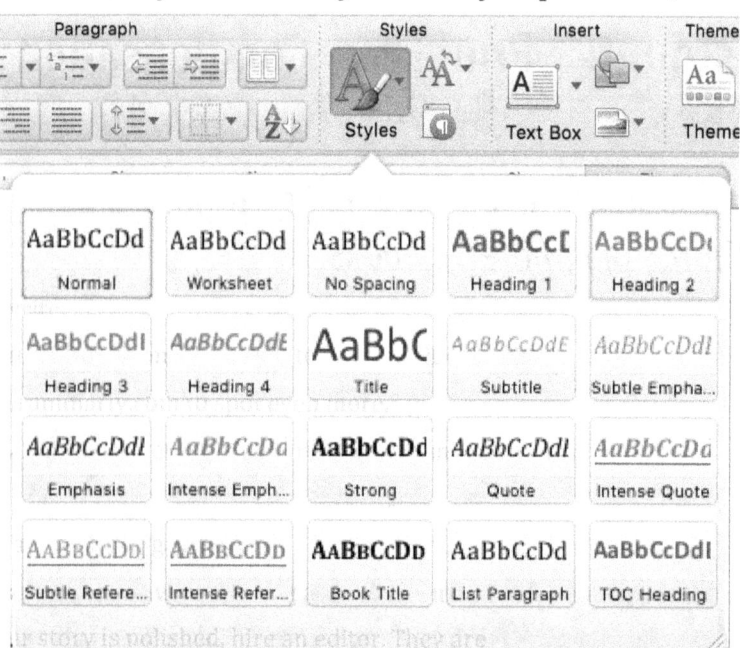

## Formatting your story

Most word processing programs allow you to assign a style to your headlines and body text. You can change the font, type size, and style of your type. If you are publishing a book, be sure to use the supplied Headlines and normal text styles so that your document can be uploaded and printed easier. It is easier to make changes to the font or type size if you use Style. In Microsoft Word, you can choose a Style such as Classic.

Thou shalt be consistent. Are you using the same font and type size for the headlines? If you're typing recipes, you want to use the same style throughout so it looks as if one person typed it, not three different people.

## Traditional printing versus print on demand

Some traditional publishers used to print about 5,000 copies of a book because it was much cheaper to print 5,000 than 100 copies. They wanted the quantity discount.

Today, some book printers are using P.O.D. (print on demand), so you can print one copy, 100 copies, or 5,000 copies, but there is no quantity discount. P.O.D. books are priced per book. With print on demand, books are not printed until someone orders a book. Amazon, IngramSpark, BookBaby, SmashBooks, and Blurb all use print on demand technology to print books. If a customer goes online and orders one book, one book is printed and shipped to them.

### Where would you purchase a book?
If you were going to buy a new book, where would you get it?

- Brick and mortar bookstore, gift shop, tourist attraction.
- Order from a bookstore's website or their in-store computer.
- Online bookstore such as Amazon, Barnes and Noble, Indigo, Book Depository, IngramSpark, and more.

### Amazon Book Sales
Amazon bought a book printing company called CreateSpace that provided print on demand (P.O.D.). Amazon also has Kindle, an electronic book reader (eBook). So, Amazon created a service called KDP (Kindle Direct Publishing) to create and sell eBooks that can be read on their Kindle readers. But now, Amazon has brought them both together under the Amazon umbrella. (I used to go online to CreateSpace to upload a P.O.D. book, but now I go to the website: KDP.Amazon.com and I can upload my book and cover and create print books or eBooks.) More information on how to upload a book for Amazon is included at the back of this book.

## IngramSpark Book Sales

Most public libraries, school libraries, bookstores, and booksellers purchase books from IngramSpark because they publish a PDF list of new books every three months and email it to 39,000 retailers and libraries all over the world.

If you pay IngramSpark for advertising, your book will be displayed in the next issue of Advance. They publish 3 different lists: Advance, Christian Advance, and Children's Advance. For $85, you can describe your book with 350 characters in Advance. My book *Robin Sees a Monster* was listed on page 158 of the Children's Advance. Or you can purchase a full-color ad in the book catalog. How will a thumbnail of your book cover look?

---

**INGRAM.**

**Robin Sees a Monster**
**From Egg to Robin**
*Barbara A. Fanson* — LSIG
It's not easy building a nest with only a beak to carry dry weeds and mud. Robin has to fight the wind while building a nest. Then she has to protect her baby birds and look for food constantly. This photographic book shares the life cycle of four robin eggs. Add two predators and it is an interesting story of survival. 46 pp. (Available now).
978-1-989361-04-7
___048114296                    paper 12.99

**Shells**
**A Pop-Up Book of Wonder**
*Janet Lawler* — JMJK
*Lindsay Dale-Scott, illustrator*
*designed by Yoojin Kim*
Along beaches, shells beckon with their timeless beauty and wonder. They provide protection for many ocean animals, populate colorful coral reefs, and sometimes surprise with a pearl inside. Fabulous interactive features and fun facts abound in this unique pop-up book. Full color. 9 x 9. 7 pp. Pub. 6/19.
978-1-62348-526-9
___040116099
29.95

**Summer Bridge Learning for Minecrafters:**
**Bridging Grades 2 to 3**
**An Unofficial Guide for Minecrafters**
*Nancy Rogers Bosse* — SYPY
*Amanda Brack, illustrator*
Colorful pages and high-interest lessons aligned with national Common Core State Standards allow young Minecrafters entering grades 2 and 3 to practice and retain key grade-level skills over the summer with zero pressure and maximum fun. Full color. 8 1/2 x 10 13/16. Consumable. 160 pp. Pub. 5/19.
978-1-51074-115-7
___043943788
paper 14.99

**Unofficial STEM Quest for Minecrafters**
**Grades 1-2**
*Stephanie J. Morris* — SYHO
This forward-thinking workbook challenges young Minecrafters to use their natural creativity and problem-solving skills to address real-world problems. Science, technology, engineering, and math come to life in each colorfully illustrated lesson that help kids discover new ways to stretch their brains, build their confidence, and satisfy their appetite for hands-on learning. 8 1/2 x 11. Consumable. 64 pp. (Available now).
978-1-51074-113-3
___043952053
paper 7.99

**W Is for Washington, DC**
*Maria Kernahan* — DYSC
*Michael Schafbuch, illustrator*
With bright, graphic illustrations and whimsical rhymes, this entry in the Alphabet Cities series takes readers on a fantastic A-Z tour of the nation's capital. Full color. 10 x 10. 56 pp. (Available now).
978-1-942402-30-5
___026776111
19.95

**What Really Matters: Emmanuel Kelly: Dream Big!**
*Mamen Sánchez* — CDLS
*Zuzanna Celej, illustrator*
*Jon Brokenbrow, translator*
Born and abandoned in war-torn Iraq, Kelly was raised at an orphanage before being adopted and taken to Australia for life-changing surgery. His sheer passion for singing, for life, and for "dreaming big" in the face of huge obstacles led him to achieve his dream of becoming a singer after he stunned judges on Australia's *The X-Factor*. Full color. 10 1/4 x 8 3/4. 24 pp. Pub. 5/19.
978-8-416-73340-8
___045744573
16.95

May/June 2019     158     For simple viewing, easy ordering, and downloading, access *Advance* online at ipage.ingramcontent.com. Choose the Browse tab, then click on Ingram Catalogs/Supplements.

# 3
# Traditional book publishing

30 years ago, traditional publishing was the only way to get your story published. After you have written your story or book, you may want your book traditionally published by another organization. There are three steps to getting a publisher: research other books, read submission guidelines, and write a query letter.

A publisher is a person or organization that finances and supervises the printing and distribution of a book. They make all the decisions regarding page design, front cover artwork, pricing the book, and how to market the book.

Some traditional publishing companies may only publish 4 to 20 books a year. Why should they publish yours?

If you get a traditional publisher to publish your book, you can focus on writing and re-writing your story. You may get 5 to 10 percent of the sales in royalty payment. The remaining book sales pay for printing, binding, marketing, administration, and distributing your books.

If you choose to self-publish your book, you keep 100% of the profits, after you pay all the expenses: arrange for editing, proofreading, illustrating, and formatting the book, printing, and market the book, so it will take longer and it will require a lot of education on your part.

## Research existing books

The first step to getting your story published by a traditional publishing company is to research other books of the same genre. Go to the public library or bookstore and look at similar books. If you're writing a children's picture book, look at other children's books. What do you like or dislike about the front cover and inside pages? A traditional book publisher will choose the right artwork for your book unless you are a professional artist.

Look to see who published the book. The publisher's information may be on the back cover or copyright page. If you wish to write a how-to book, find a publisher who specializes in instructional manuals or books.

## Check the publisher's website

Are they accepting unsolicited manuscripts? What are their submission guidelines? Follow their instructions carefully. If you can't, why should they work with you? What other books have they published? Do you like their front covers and distribution? If they ask for a photo, give them one; follow their guidelines carefully.

## Write a query letter

Take your time and research other letters. This is your letter of introduction, so you want to make a good first impression.

There are four key sections in the one-page query letter:

- The introduction and hook
- The book description (like you would put on a back cover)
- Author biography
- A call to action with contact information.

Agents or publishers are looking to see if the book is marketable, so avoid being too witty. It is more important to demonstrate your book's niche than your sense of humor. But, keep it short to 200 – 400 words.

The second part of the query letter is the story or summary. How would you describe the story on the back cover of the book? Can you add a cliffhanger so the publisher will want to read more? You can have two or three paragraphs to describe the setting, tension, and plot, but avoid trying to introduce every character.

The author's bio should not be your complete résumé. Just focus on the relevant information. Have you published any stories before in books, magazines, or newspapers? Do you have a relevant degree or attend a writer's conference? What makes you qualified to write a book? Do you belong to an association or have connections to assist in book sales?

The final paragraph of your query letter should be methods of contacting you. Include a telephone number, address, and email address. If you have an author website, let them know. If you have a social media page promoting another book or your future book, let them know. Show that you're committed to promoting yourself and your book. Have you done speaking engagements in the past? But, only show social media links if the page is maintained.

## Query Sample 1

Hi [Name of Editor],

I have a story that I believe [Publisher] will like, and I'd be honored if you'd consider it for publication.

My story "[Name of article]" is a [genre]. I will [more about your book here].

A little about me: [Bio here]

I have included a sample. You can telephone me: _____ or email me: _____.

Sincerely,

[Your name]

## Query Sample 2

Hi Ann,

I have a story called *Robin Sees a Monster* that I believe you will find interesting and informative. I hope you will consider it for publication.

*Robin Sees a Monster* is a children's picture book about protecting babies.

A little about me: I'm a graphic designer, author, and retired college professor who enjoys hiking and photography. See more on my website: Fanson.net.

Please let me know how I can help you. Telephone 905-679-9229 or email: Barbara@Fanson.net.

Sincerely,

Barbara A. Fanson

# 4
# Self-Publishing a book

## Hybrid Publishing

Hybrid Publishing is when you hire a company with publishing experience to produce a good quality book for you. The author retains most of the creative control and a share in the profit but pays for services rendered by the publisher. The hybrid publisher provides help, support, and guidance to get your book off a printing press and into the hands of readers. You pay for whatever services you need.

Most hybrid publishers are paid in advance for services rendered and then you get paid a portion of the royalties. Emerald Lake Books keeps 50%. Like traditional publishers, many hybrid publishers are selective and don't accept just any manuscript.

The Independent Book Publishers Association (IBPA) has a list of nine criteria they want hybrid publishers to follow:

- Define a mission and vision for its publishing program.
- Vet submissions.
- Publish under its imprint(s) and ISBNs.
- Publish to industry standards
- Ensure editorial, design, and production quality.
- Pursue and manage a range of publishing rights.
- Provide distribution services.
- Demonstrate respectable sales.
- Pay authors a higher-than-standard royalty.

## Vanity Publishers

Unfortunately, some hybrid publishers are called vanity publishers. They will take your story, produce what the author wants, and disappear after the book is published. Sometimes, the book has a substandard quality that's difficult to sell. These are the hybrid publishers that give legitimate publishers a bad reputation.

So, make sure you're dealing with a reputable firm, check Google for reviews, testimonials, and follow the IBPA standards listed above. Ask to see samples or go to a bookstore and look for some of their books so you can see the quality for yourself. You could also mail one of their clients and ask for a reference.

## Publish a book yourself

From this section onwards, it's assumed you want to print and distribute books yourself. Some businesses are now using books like a business card. Other people want to print copies of their genealogical research. Maybe you want to share family recipes. Or you have an idea for a seminar that other people will find interesting.

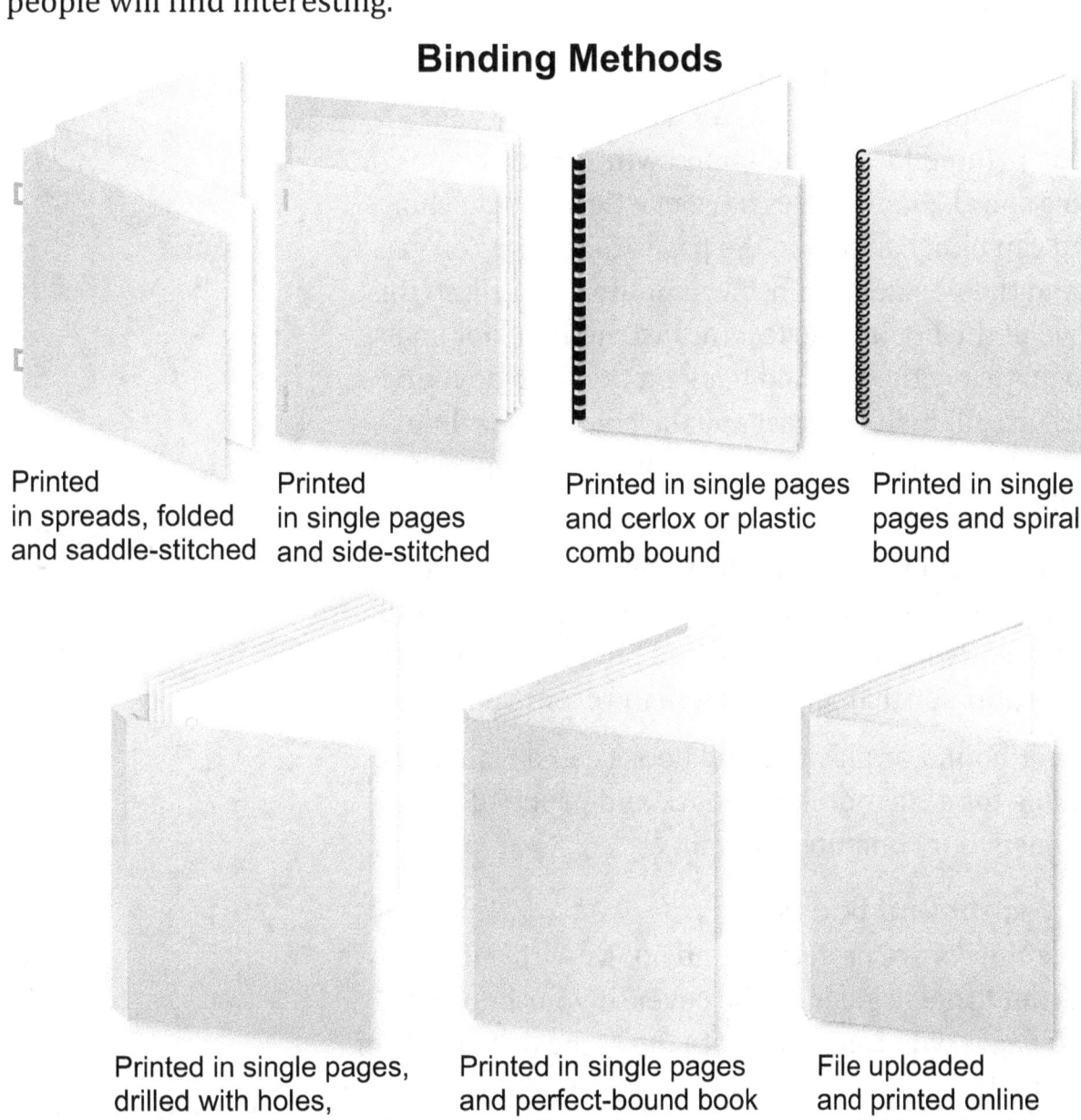

**Binding Methods**

Printed in spreads, folded and saddle-stitched

Printed in single pages and side-stitched

Printed in single pages and cerlox or plastic comb bound

Printed in single pages and spiral bound

Printed in single pages, drilled with holes, and bound in binder

Printed in single pages and perfect-bound book by bindery shop

File uploaded and printed online and shipped to you

*Barbara A. Fanson*

# Different styles of books

What is a book? According to Merriam-Webster, a book is "a set of written, printed, or blank sheets bound together between a front and back cover."

"A book is a bound collection of pages," suggests author Barbara Fanson.

What type of book do you want to produce? The style of book you choose will determine the printing and binding price.

## Plastic comb or wire spiral

You can add more pages later. You can have your book printed locally and bound with plastic combs or wire spiral. Many offices have plastic comb machines and can punch and bind the pages together. You can stand the book up against a computer or wall, so this style of the book is perfect for instructional manuals. Do not leave the finished book on the dash of your car—it will melt and reshape the comb. Over time and lots of use, the plastic comb will not open as well to add more pages.

Spiral-bound books offer the same features as the plastic comb, but look a little more professional and last slightly longer. Spiral-bound books have become more popular than plastic comb in recent years.

Spiral-bound or plastic comb books can be laid flat on a table for a class or folded back and propped up against your computer or wall.

## Perfect-bound books

Most novels are perfect-bound books with a flat left side and sheets glued to the cover. If your book has 100 pages, you can add text to the spine or flat side of the book.

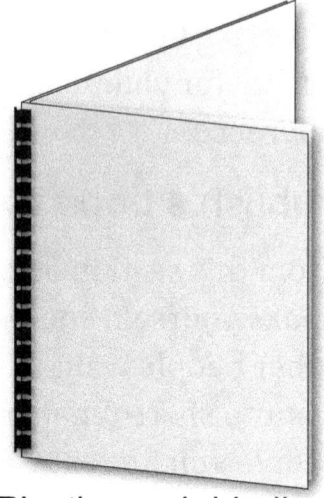

Plastic comb binding

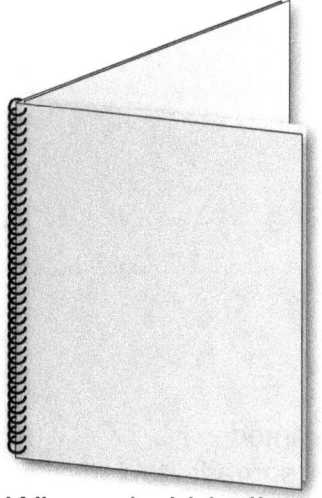

Wire spiral binding

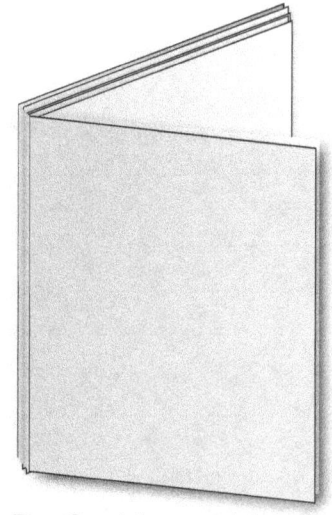

Perfect-bound book

## Binder with loose-leaf paper
A binder is an excellent binding option for seminars or collections. If you think people will collect bulletins regularly, then a binder is ideal. If you're planning a class or seminar, a binder lets you add pages or adapt the book as the class changes. A monthly newsletter can be collected and saved in a binder.

The binder can have pockets or a clear plastic cover so you can insert a cover page. If you have a plastic sleeve on the side, you can add a small insert for spine text.

## Saddle-stitched books
A saddle-stitched book is ideal for 48 pages or less. The larger pages are folded and then 2 or 3 staples are added.

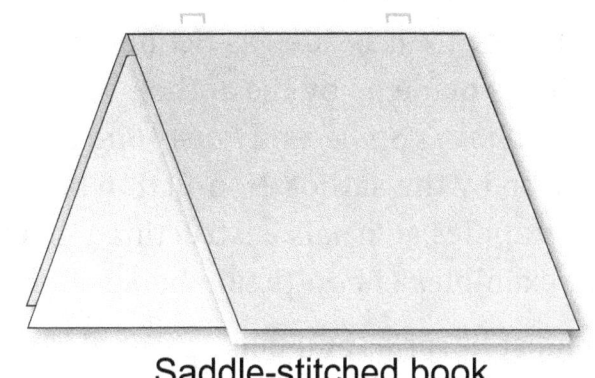
Saddle-stitched book

## Side-stitched books
Side-stitched books are for single pages that are not folded. 2 or 3 staples are added to the front cover, which goes through the pages to the back.

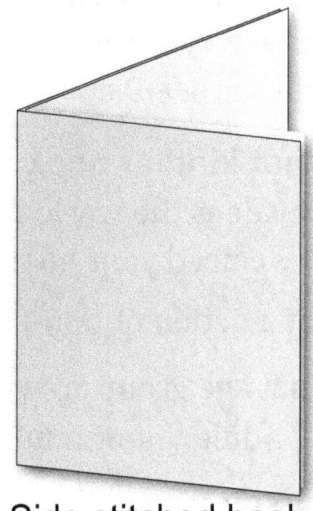
Side-stitched book

## Z-fold books or maps
Z-Card® Canada in Brampton specializes in z-fold books and promotions. This is perfect for maps or tourist brochures. The finished product fits into a tourist's pocket but can be unfolded to show the big picture or map.

There is usually a cardstock front and back cover, which is glued to the larger, folded page. You can even have a slit cut into the cardstock to hold a hotel room card, business card, or loyalty card.

## Activity booklets
Booklets can be made by taking a large sheet of paper and folding it so it resembles a book. Booklets are ideal for activity pages or take-away items.

*Barbara A. Fanson*

## eBooks

Electronic books or eBooks are digital books that can be read on electronic devices like Amazon's Kindle, Kobo Reader, Nook, iBooks, and PDFs on a computer screen or tablet. eBooks can be read, saved, borrowed, and deleted without using a single tree for paper. You can take a hundred books on vacation without carrying an extra suitcase.

## Different types of books

All books are classified as fiction or non-fiction. Fiction books contain a story, which is made up by the author. *To Kill a Mockingbird, Harry Potter & the Philosopher's Stone,* and *Paper Bag Princess* are popular fiction books that are written by the author. Non-fiction books contain facts and information. Biographies, journals, instructional manuals, travel books, and "how-to" books are examples of non-fiction books. Books are divided into sub-types or genres.

In most libraries and bookstores, fiction books are shelved alphabetically by the author's last name. Non-fiction books are assigned a number according to the Dewey Decimal System. For example, cookbooks are 641 and history books are 940s.

## What kind of book are you publishing?

Why does the world need one more book? There are millions of books ... why do we need your book? _____

Is it a fiction or non-fiction book? _____

What age group are you targeting? _____
    Adult, young adult, children, tweens

Classifications _____

# Book Genres

## Children
Action
Adventure
Animals
Coming of Age
Concept
Educational
Fable
Fantasy/Sci-Fi
General
Grades 4 – 6
Grades K – 2
Mystery
Mythology/Fairy Tale
Non-Fiction
Picture Book
Preschool
Preteen
Religious Theme
Social Issues

## Christian
Amish
Biblical Counseling
Children
Devotion/Study
Fantasy/Sci-Fi
Fiction
General
Historical Fiction
Living
Non-Fiction
Romance - Contemporary
Romance - General
Romance - Historical
Thriller

## Fiction
Action
Adventure
Animals
Anthology
Audiobook
Chick Lit
Crime
Cultural
Drama
Dystopia
Fantasy - Epic
Fantasy - General
Fantasy - Urban
General
Graphic Novel/Comic
Historical - Event/Era
Historical - Personage
Holiday
Honor
Humor/Comedy
Inspirational
Intrigue
Literary
Magic/Wizardry
Military
Mystery - General
Mystery - Historical
Mystery - Legal
Mystery - Murder
Mystery - Sleuth
Mythology
New Adult
Paranormal
Realistic
Religious Theme
Science Fiction
Short Story/Novella
Social Issues
Southern
Sports
Supernatural
Suspense
Tall Tale
Thriller - Conspiracy
Thriller - General
Thriller - Legal
Thriller - Medical
Thriller - Political
Thriller - Psychological
Thriller - Terrorist
Time Travel
Urban
Visionary
Western
Women's

## Non-Fiction
Adventure
Animals
Anthology
Art/Photography
Audiobook
Autobiography
Biography
Business/Finance
Cooking/Food
Cultural
Drama
Education
Environment
Genealogy
General
Gov./Politics
Grief/Hardship
Health - Fitness
Health - Medical
Historical
Hobby
Home/Crafts
Humor/Comedy
Inspirational
Memoir
Military
Motivational
Music/Entertainment
New Age
Occupational
Parenting
Relationships
Religion/Philosophy
Retirement
Self Help
Short Story/Novella
Social Issues
Spiritual or Supernatural
Sports
Travel
True Crime
Women's
Writing/Publishing

## Poetry
General
Inspirational
Love/Romance

Romance
Comedy
Contemporary
Fantasy/Sci-Fi
General
Historical
Paranormal
Sizzle
Suspense

## Young Adult
Action
Adventure
Coming of Age
Fantasy - Epic
Fantasy - General
Fantasy - Urban
General
Horror
Mystery
Mythology/Fairy Tale

## Non-Fiction
Paranormal
Religious Theme
Romance
Sci-Fi
Social Issues
Th

# 5
# Do you need illustrations or photographs?

If you are having the book published by a traditional publisher, they will supply the artwork for the covers. If you are self-publishing the book, you will need a high-resolution, full-color photograph or illustration for the front cover. You can have an abstract image on the cover with large type, but what do other books in your genre have on the front cover?

John Green is a New York Times best selling author.

Several of his books including *The Fault in Our Stars* have a simple type and basic colored shapes on the front cover.

*Milestones & Memories* has a yellow and green cover. The hardest part of designing the cover was finding an image for the baby record book **and beyond**. I didn't want to show a baby because the book is for recording milestones throughout their life into adulthood.

How will your book look in black and white? Or small?

## Add Alt Text to images

Images should have Alt Text—a description of the image for peple who may have vision problems. If a book is read to a vision-impaired individual, they will be told the Alt Text.

To add Alt Text in Microsoft Word, right-click on your image and choose Format Picture. A dialog box appears. From the list on the left, choose Alt Text. Provide a title and a short description.

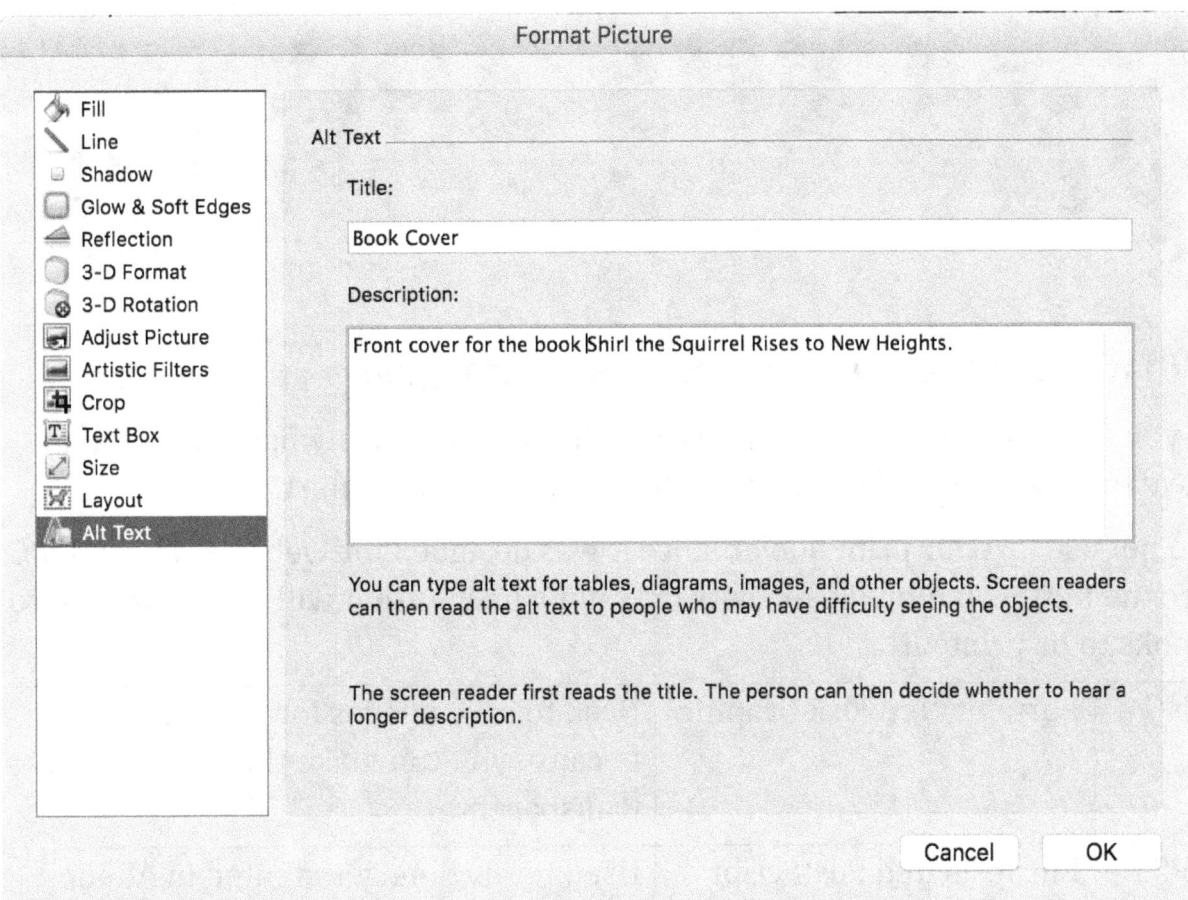

Add Alt Text to tables, diagrams, images, and other artwork so that screen readers can read it to people who may have difficulty seeing the objects. The screen reader reads the title first and then the person can decide whether to hear a longer description.

In Adobe InDesign, you can also add Alt Text. With an image selected in InDesign, choose Object > Object Export

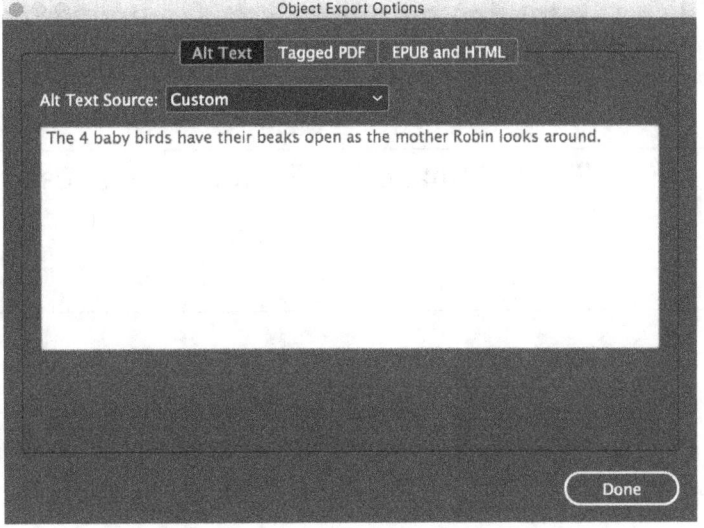

*Barbara A. Fanson*

Options. A dialog box appeared. Click on the Alt Text button at the top and type a title for the image. Then, click on the Done button.

## What file format should you use for images?

If your book contains photographs, graphs, tables, or drawings, you should save them with a file format that other programs can import.

Do not use PNG for print books, since it was designed for web use. TIF and JPG are the most common file formats for saving images that will be imported into books to be printed.

| PNG | Portable Network Graphic | Used to save images for web design because you can make the background transparent. |
|---|---|---|
| EPS | Encapsulated PostScript | Used to save images created in Adobe Illustrator for print products like books. |
| JPEG | Joint Photographic Experts Group | Images from cameras are often saved as JPEGs or JPGs, but lose data because images are compressed. |
| TIFF | Tagged Image File Format | Images for print are often saved as TIFF or TIF, since it does not lose data when compressed. |

# 6
# Should the book have a bleed or no bleed?

## Book margins
Margins are the white space around the page edges. You don't want text to go too close to the edge and accidentally get cut off, so we add margins around the edges of the paper.

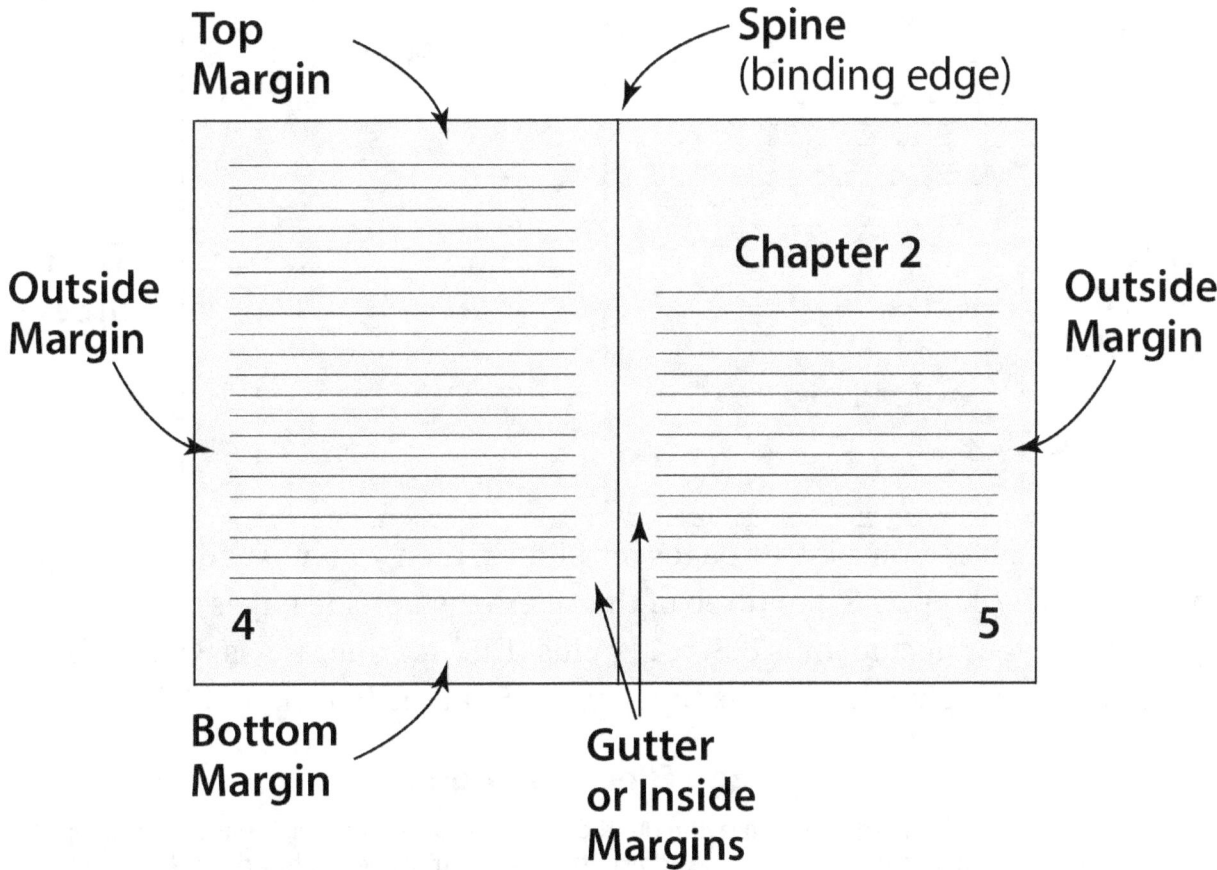

## Will your book have a bleed?
Bleed is a printing term that refers to printing that goes beyond the edge of the paper before trimming. When a book is trimmed to size, the excess ink gets cut off. For example, if you wanted a business card to have a color photograph or colored box to go right up to the edge, you would make the photograph bigger than the card. When the card gets trimmed to a standard size of 3½" x 2", the excess photo—or colored ink—would get trimmed off. Most print shops want you to add a bleed of ⅛" or .125".

Can you imagine a print shop trying to print that photograph right up to the trim edge of a card. What if they're a smidgen short? A slither of white paper might show on the edge. So, it is easier for a print shop to print on larger paper and then trim it.

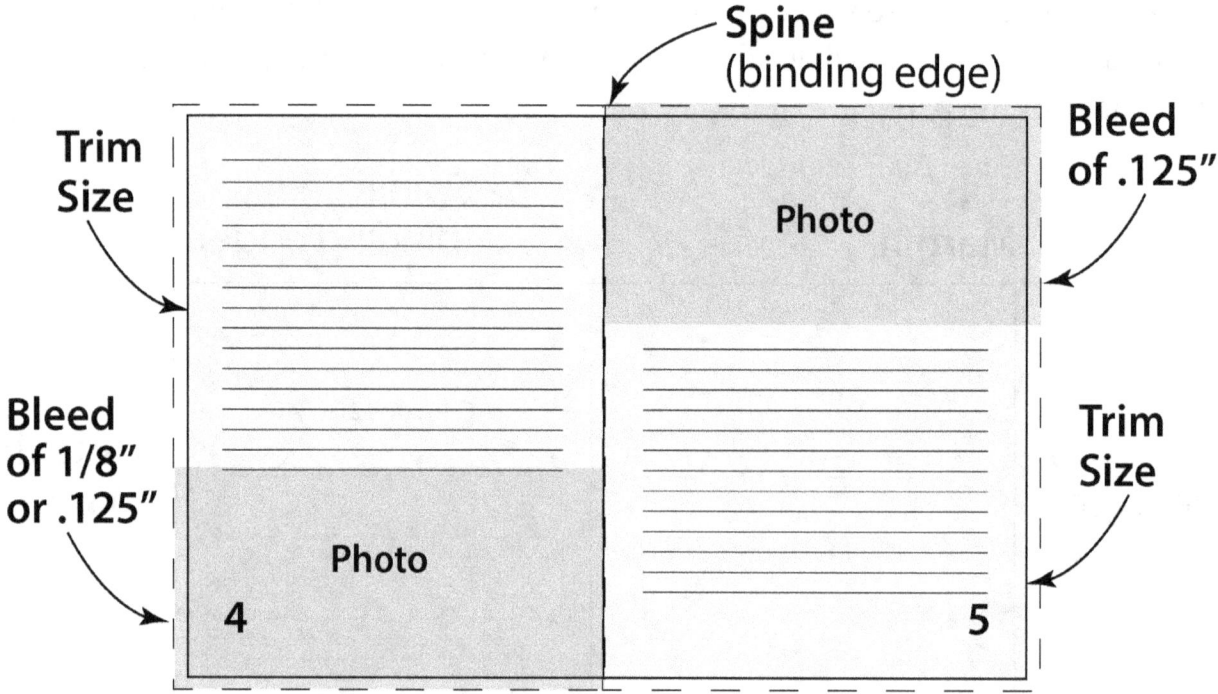

If you want a bleed on all your pages for photos, then you must add an eighth of an inch (.1/8" or .125") to three of the sides (the outside edges). For example, if your document is 8.5" x 11" plus .125" for one side is 8.625". The page is 11" long plus .125" at the top, plus .125" at the bottom is 11.25".

### A Page Bleed Enlarged

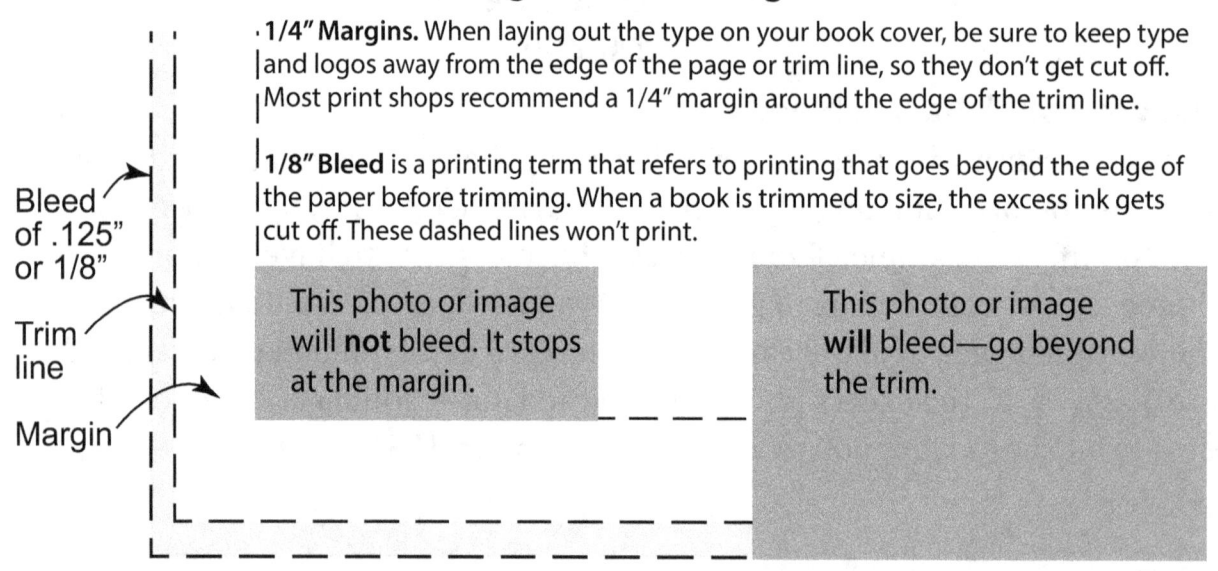

# 7
# Designing a book cover

What should you include on the front cover? Go to the library or local bookstore and research other books in similar genres. Do they have an image on the front or just type? At the very minimum, the front cover should have the title of the book, the author's name, and if this is part of a series, list it. If someone enjoyed the first *Shirl the Squirrel Adventure*, they may enjoy the next one, too. At the bottom of the front cover, it says *A Shirl the Squirrel Adventure*. Also, if children saw your book at an author visit or in their school library, they may recognize it and want to buy this book, too.

If your book has a subtitle, you should show that on the front cover and the copyright page. *Preserving Dundas* is the book title and *Building memories one photo at a time* is the subtitle.

It's not easy building a nest with only a beak to carry dry weeds and mud. Robin has to fight the wind while building a nest. Then she has to protect her baby birds and look for food constantly.

From egg to Robin, this photographic book shares the life cycle of four robin eggs. Add two predators and you have an interesting story of survival.

Children will enjoy this engaging and entertaining book while exploring the eating habits of robins, making a nest, watching baby robins grow, and dealing with predators like cats and raccoons.

*"Her books are well loved by the students. Her presentation is engaging, educational, and the students loved it!!"*
Kathleen Malarczuk, Teacher-Librarian, HWCDSB

## Designing the back cover

When people look at a book in the bookstore, they often look at the front cover, then the back cover, and then they might read the first page. Your back cover should have a short book description—a summary to entice people to buy your book.

Often books have a photo, short author's bio, author's photo, and quotations from reviewers on the back cover.

If your book will be sold in bookstores, then you should have an ISBN and barcode on the back cover. The back cover of *Robin Sees a Monster* has a large photo with two descriptions—one in a box on the photo and one under the photo. There is a quotation from

**Tragedy on the Twenty**

*Can you imagine raising four children under four during the depression—without a husband?*

The Toronto Maple Leafs are in the Stanley Cup Playoffs for the second year in a row. Will they defeat the New York Rangers to win the coveted cup two years in a row? Famous bank robbers Bonnie and Clyde have another shoot-out with police. Will they get caught this time? German Chancellor Adolph Hitler is making changes in Germany that make the rest of the world start to wonder.

A horrible accident on Highway 20 quickly becomes the talk of the town. This historical fiction book examines the newspaper clippings and the inquest during April 1933. Tragedy on the Twenty explores how the family dealt with the accident, hospital visits, running a store during the Depression, planning a funeral, attending the inquest, and beyond. With three children under four—and a fourth on the way—Janetta Fanson wonders how she'll raise her children with no job or driver's license during the worst year of the depression.

Barbara Fanson is a graphic designer, author and Janetta's granddaughter. She has written over 30 books, but this is her first historical fiction book.

*"A great read. Enjoyed it thoroughly. A good read for all ages."*
—D. Gaudette

a school librarian under the second description. This book has an author's bio, but not a photo of the author. The barcode has an ISBN (International Standard Book Number) and the price of the book.

The back cover of *Tragedy on the Twenty* has a small photo, a book description, an author's bio and photo, and a barcode. This book also has a QR code in the bottom-left corner. When scanned by an app on your cellphone, you will see the author's or publisher's website. You can get free QR codes but they probably have limited time and may expire

Many self-publishers will hire a graphic designer to design the front, back, and spine artwork. A printing company will want flat camera-ready artwork with a bleed—artwork that extends at least 1/8' past the trim marks.

For the front or back cover, photographs and illustrations must be high-resolution CMYK. High-resolution means that at the time you took the photo, your camera should have been set with a high-resolution of 300

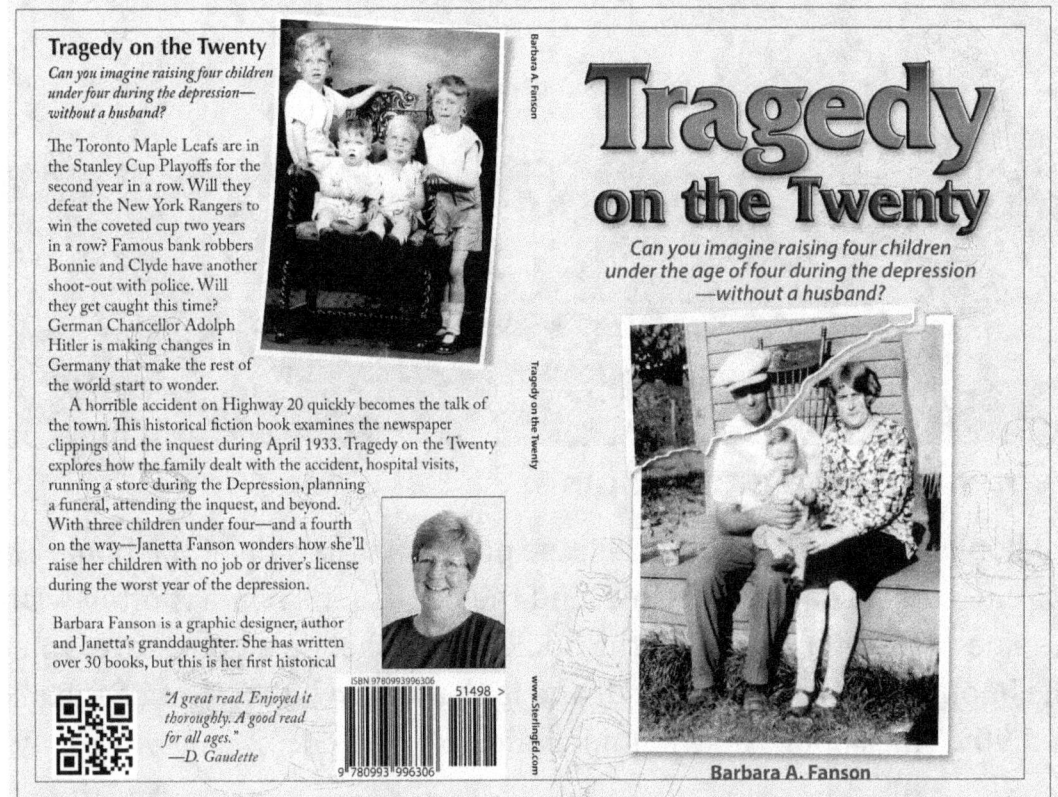

pixels per inch (ppi) or higher. Or, if you're scanning a photograph or drawing into your computer, make sure the scanning software is set to 300 ppi or higher so you're are digitizing the image with 300 pixels per inch. If you're drawing illustrations in a software program like Adobe Illustrator, start with a high resolution. CMYK are printers' colors: cyan, magenta, yellow, and black.

Text on the spine of books is often rotated 90° so if the book is laid down, it can still be read.

Thick books could have text that is not rotated.

The second book from the left is a creative children's book with text going downward vertically.

## Can you have type on the spine?

Not all books can have type on the spine or text on the side of the book. The title of the book, the author's name, and the publisher's name is often written on the side of the book so that if the book is on a shelf in a bookstore, you can see the book title. Do your research and look at some books. Notice the text is rotated 90°. Thick books may not need the text rotated.

Using the IngramSpark Cover above, your background colors or images should cover the dark grey area. All text and important images should be inside the light grey area.

If your book is perfect bound, you may be able to add type to the spine if you have a certain number of pages. But, the number of pages varies with printers.

Amazon's KDP wants at least 100 pages before you can add text to the spine. You can use their KDP's Cover Creator to help design a cover, but you **cannot** export a copy of it to use elsewhere. You may wish to upload your book elsewhere or use the book artwork in your promotions.

IngramSpark prefers a minimum of 48 pages to qualify for spine text. It is challenging to center text on a spine if it is really thin. They say 48 pages, but I couldn't have spine text on a 64-page book because they want 1/8" or 3 mm of space around the text.

Ingram has a Cover Template Generator available for Adobe InDesign or PDF that designers can use to design cover artwork. The custom template is created for your book based on the number of pages, trim size, binding method, and other information that you provide. You can re-use the artwork in your promotions.

## Extra artwork for case bound or hardcover books

If you are planning to print hardcover books or case bound books, you will need another ½" of background color. The original bleed of 1/8" plus ½" = .625" of extra color since the cover will wrap around and be glued to the inside of the book.

## Add a dust jacket

Many book printers can add a dust jacket or paper wrap around your book for an additional fee. There are 5 parts to a dust jacket: back flap, back cover, spine, front cover, and front flap. The flaps are usually 3" wide. Artwork should be supplied as a separate PDF file showing all 5 parts.

## 5 parts of a dust jacket

| Back Flap | Back Cover | Spine | Front Cover | Front Flap |

But, do not add borders or lines around your parts or they will print.

*Barbara A. Fanson*

# 8
# Book Trim Size

The trim size is the size of the finished book—after it has been printed, bound, and trimmed.

Take a ruler to the public library and look at other books in the same genre as your book to see what the most popular size is. While you're at the library, you can see which company published the book and what size they prefer.

Figure 3: Books come in a variety of sizes.

## Children's Books
The most popular trim sizes for children's books: 7.5"x7.5", 7"x10", or 10"x8".

## Paperbacks or novels
Paperbacks or novels that are mostly text are either 6"x9" or 5"x8", though they could be any size.

## Non-fiction books
Non-fiction books come in a variety of sizes such as 8.5"x11", 6"x9", and 8"x8".

Most print-on-demand book printers have similar sizes. IngramSpark's most popular book sizes range from 4"x6" to 11"x8.5". The first number is always the width of the book.

## IngramSpark's Book Trim Sizes

| Paperback Books | Hardcover Books |
|---|---|
| Trade paperback books, available with perfect binding: <br> 4 x 6" (154 x 102mm) <br> 4 x 7" (178 x 102mm) <br> 4.25 x 7" (178 x 108mm) <br> 4.37 x 7" (178 x 111mm) A <br> 4.72 x 7.48" (190 x 120mm) <br> 5 x 7" (178 x 127mm) <br> 5 x 8" (203 x 127mm) <br> 5.06 x 7.81" (198 x 129mm) <br> 5.25 x 8" (203 x 133mm) <br> 5.5 x 8.25" (210 x 140mm) <br> 5.5 x 8.5" (216 x 140mm) <br> 5.83 x 8.27" (210 x 148mm) A5 <br> 6 x 9" (229 x 152mm) <br> 6.14 x 9.21" (234 x 156mm) <br> 6.5 x 6.5" (165 x 165mm) <br> 6.625 x 10.25" (260 x 168mm) (Graphic Novel) <br> 6.69 x 9.61" (244 x 170mm) (Pinched Crown) <br> 7 x 10" (254 x 178mm) <br> 7.44 x 9.69" (246 x 189mm) <br> 7.5 x 9.25" (235 x 191mm) <br> 8 x 8" (203 x 203mm) <br> 8 x 10" (254 x 203mm) <br> 8 x 10.88" (276 x 203mm) <br> 8.25 x 10.75" (273 x 210mm) <br> 8.25 x 11" (279 x 210mm) <br> 8.268 x 11.693" (297 x 210mm) A4 <br> 8.5 x 8.5" (216 x 216mm) <br> 8.5 x 9" (229 x 216mm) <br> 8.5 x 11" (280 x 216mm) <br> 11 x 8.5" (216 x 280mm) Premium Color Only | Hardcover books are available in case laminate with no jacket or cloth, with or without a jacket. <br> 5 x 8" (203 x 127mm) Case Lam/Cloth/Jacket <br> 5.5 x 8.5" (216 x 140mm) Case Lam/Cloth/Jacket <br> 5.83 x 8.27" (210 x 148mm) Case Lam <br> 6 x 9" (229 x 152mm) Case Lam/Cloth/Jacket <br> 6.14 x 9.21" (234 x 156mm) Case Lam/Cloth/Jacket <br> 6.69 x 9.61" (244 x 170mm) Case Lam <br> 7 x 10" (254 x 178mm) Case Lam <br> 7.5 x 9.25" (235 x 191mm) Case Lam <br> 8 x 8" (203 x 203mm) Case Lam <br> 8 x 10" (254 x 203mm) Case Lam <br> 8 x 10.88" (276 x 203mm) Case Lam <br> 8.25 x 10.75" (273 x 210mm) Case Lam <br> 8.5 x 8.5" (216 x 216mm) Case Lam <br> 8.5 x 11" (280 X 216mm) Case Lam <br> 11 x 8.5" (216 x 280mm) Case Lam, Premium Color Only |

## KDP's Book Trim Sizes

| Paperback Books |
|---|
| 5" x 8" (12.7 x 20.32 cm) <br> 5.06" x 7.91" (12.85 x19.84 cm) <br> 5.25" x 8" (13.34 x 20.32 cm) <br> 5.5" x 8.5" (13.97 x 21.59 cm) |

6" x 9" (15.24 x 22.86 cm)
6.14" x 9.21" (15.6 x 23.39 cm)
6.69" x 9.61" (16.99 x 24.4 cm)
7" x 10" (17.78 x 25.4 cm)
7.44" x 9.69" (18.9 x 24.61 cm)
7.5" x 9.25" (19.05 x 23.5 cm)
8" x 10" (20.32 x 25.4 cm)
8.5" x 11" (21.59 x 27.94 cm)
8.25" x 6" (20.96 x 15.24 cm)
8.25" x 8.25" (20.96 x 20.96 cm)
8.27" x 11.69" (21 x 29.7 cm)
8.5" x 8.5" (21.59 x 21.59 cm)

# Comparison of three printers

|  | **Ingram** | **Amazon's KDP** | **BookBaby** |
|---|---|---|---|
| Set-up fee | $49 | 0 | $299 Global |
| Number of pages for spine text | At least 48 pages | At least 100 pages | |
| Cover Artwork | Cover Template Generator can be used for your promotions | Cover Creator cannot be exported and used in promotions | They supply PDF template, which can be opened in several programs. |
| Hard Cover | Yes, Case Bound | No | |
| 100 copies, 40 pages | $286.99 + $25 Print on Demand | $386.00 Print on Demand | $1,078.00 Printing Press |
| Std. Shipping 100 books | $60.69 | $60.00 | $58.49 |
| 60 lb. white paper, matte | Plus $25 set-up | | |

GLOBAL CONNECT/ESPRESSO SALES REPORT
Sterling Education Centre Inc. (9111981)
United States Operating Unit - USD Transactions
For Period of JUN-19
Run Date: 06-JUL-2019
Period: 01-JUN-2019 To 30-JUN-2019
Page: 1

| Title | Author(s) | List Price | Disc | Wholesale Price | Quantity | Net Sales | Print Charge | Net Pub Comp |
|---|---|---|---|---|---|---|---|---|
| Shirl the Squirrel Rises to June Global - India Sales Bookstore | Fanson, | 14.99 | 55% | 6.75 | 1 | 6.75 | -4.14 | 2.61 |

Since bookstores, libraries, and schools can purchase the book with a discount of 55%, they pay $6.75 for each book, rather than the book price of $14.99. Less the printing of $4.14, the author receives $2.61 per book or 17%.

My other traditional book publisher pays me 10% for each book sale.

## Will the interior pages be color or black and white?

It is cheaper to print black and white interior pages, just like black and white photocopies are cheaper than color photocopies. So make sure all your text and images are black or grayscale (shades of black).

Children's picture books and some educational books should have full-color illustrations or photographs.

Do you want the inside or interior pages printed on white paper or natural beige paper? Do you want glossy paper?

Sometimes the images fill the page and sometimes there is a margin around the outside of the page. If you are **not** sure how to create a bleed—where the image is at least 1/8" bigger than the page and then trimmed off after printing—then stick with a margin.

The left page has a bleed—the background image goes all the way to the edge and the page number is printed right over the image. The right page has a white margin around the edge of the page with the page number printed in the white margin.

## Where can you get good quality images?

If you wish to have a photograph or illustration on the front cover, here are some suggestions:

- Ask an illustrator or photograph for an appropriate image. Pay upfront for the image or by royalty. Make sure you also have the right to use the image in book promotions. You should have a contract and only use the image for this book and it's promotions, not for anything else.
Do they need credit on the Copyright page? If they all providing multiple images throughout the book, then they should be listed on the front cover: Illustrations by Barbara Fanson, or whatever.
- Ask a college student who is studying photography or illustration. It's a chance for them to create a piece for their portfolio.
- Fiverr.com connects people with illustrators and photographers at a fee you both agree upon.
- Pixabay.com has photographs and illustrations for non-commercial use, but if you wish to use them in a book, there is a fee.
- Online stock photography websites will let you download one image or many images for a fee such as Shutterstock.com, CanStock.com, Dreamstime.com, BigStockPhoto.com, and iStockPhoto.com.
- People used to purchase stock images on a CD, but that's not as popular as before.

## Vector Graphics versus Raster Graphics

The letter 'a' was typed with 24 pt. Adobe Caslon Pro, and then enlarged 1600% to show the difference between two software programs.

**Adobe Illustrator** on the left, is a vector graphics drawing program. It uses Bézier curves and anchor points to create artwork that can be enlarged or reduced without ruining the art.

**Adobe Photoshop** and Paint programs are raster graphic software programs that use pixels that are dependent on resolution. Artwork and images created in Photoshop should be created the size you want and not enlarged later.

# 9
# Prepare your book for upload

Fill in this worksheet after you have finished formatting your book and before you upload it online.

Title _____

    Enter your title as it appears on the book cover and copyright page.

Subtitle _____

    A subtitle is a subordinate title that contains additional information about the content of the book. You do not have to have a subtitle. KDP prefers fewer than 200 characters for the title and subtitle.

Series _____

    A series is a set of connected books. If your book is **not** a part of a series, leave this blank. A series number will help readers find other books in the series.

Edition Number _____

    Is this a revised or updated book? If you just corrected some typos, it is not a new version.

Language _____

    What language is used in the book? English, French, Spanish, etc.

Primary Author _____

Contributors _____

    Credit other authors, illustrators, and photographers but this is optional.

Publisher _____

    If you are the book's author or publisher, enter your name or your company. KDP is not the publisher; they just support authors.

Description _____

_____

_____

_____

Genre _____
> Fiction, non-fiction, children's picture book, historical fiction book, memoir, children's education book, young adult mystery, etc.

Keywords _____

Categories _____

Age and grade range _____

ISBN _____

Imprint Name _____

Publication Date _____

Ink ☐         Black & White Interior Pages     ☐ Color Interior Pages

Paper Type _____

Trim Size _____

## Add an ISBN and Barcode to Your Book

### ISBN (International Standard Book Number)

You will need an ISBN (International Standard Book Number) for each format of your book: hardcover, softcover, eBook, etc. You must own your ISBN.

Any book printed by IngramSpark must have a barcode showing the ISBN (International Standard Book Number). In Canada, you can get an ISBN free from the government of Canada. https://www.collectionscanada.gc.ca

In the U. S. you can buy an ISBN from Bowker.

### Get ISBN from Collections Canada

On the CollectionsCanada.gc.ca website, create a login and password.

1. From the list on the left, choose Request ISBN.
2. Change Product Form from Book to whatever your media is.
3. Type the Title of your book or whatever.
4. Enter the Projected Publication Date. Is your book forthcoming? If not, you can change the status to Active or Cancelled or whatever.

5. Add a Note if you wish.
6. If you check the Send ISBN Confirmation by Email box, you will get an automatically generated email showing your ISBN.
7. Click on the Save button. A different page will show.
8. Click on the View Logbook link to see all your books and their ISBNs.
9. If you click on the link for the ISBN, you can edit the publication (or copy the ISBN). Don't forget to log out.

## Barcode

Any book printed by IngramSpark must have a barcode showing the ISBN (International Standard Book Number). If you are using IngramSpark to create the artwork for the covers, they can make a barcode with your ISBN. The barcode

*ISBNs issued after 2007 have 13 digits. Each version of your book should have its own unique number.*

will be on the PDF that the Cover Generator sends by email. You can move the barcode. (See next page for more details about Cover Generator.)

If you want to sell your book in bookstores, you may wish to show the book's fee included in the barcode.

If you're getting your book printed by Amazon, you can purchase a barcode. There are free Barcode Generators that you can find on the Internet. http://www.barcode-generator.org

## Designing a Cover

To create a cover for your book, you have four choices:

1. Create your cover in Adobe Illustrator, Photoshop, or InDesign.
2. Hire someone to create the artwork for you.
3. Generate a cover online through Amazon (KDP).
4. Use the IngramSpark Cover Generator and receive a PDF by email.

## IngramSpark's Cover Generator

To upload a book cover to IngramSpark, use their custom Cover Generator tool, located in the Tools section of their website. Just fill in the required fields and a custom template will be emailed to you. You can keep the cover artwork and use it anytime, anywhere. The PDF will be one piece of artwork for the back cover, front cover, and spine.

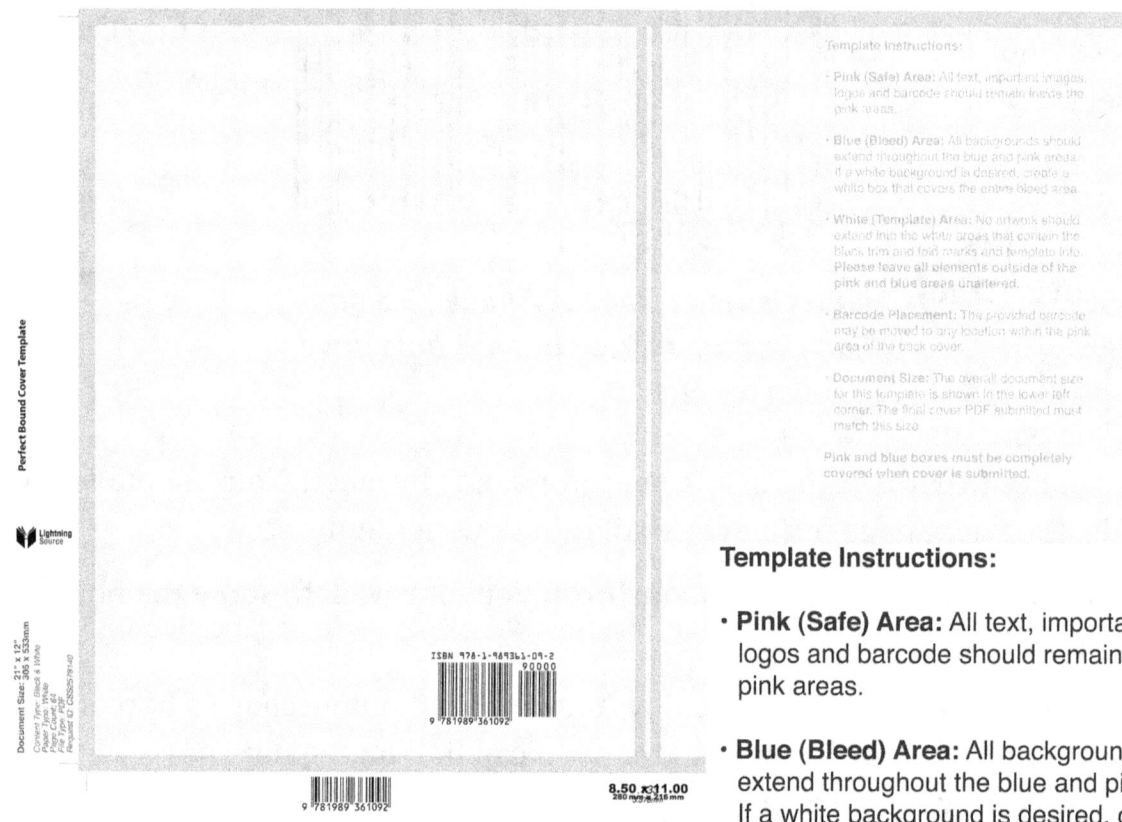

**Template Instructions:**

- **Pink (Safe) Area:** All text, important images, logos and barcode should remain inside the pink areas.

- **Blue (Bleed) Area:** All backgrounds should extend throughout the blue and pink areas. If a white background is desired, create a white box that covers the entire bleed area.

- **White (Template) Area:** No artwork should extend into the white areas that contain the black trim and fold marks and template info. **Please leave all elements outside of the pink and blue areas unaltered.**

- **Barcode Placement:** The provided barcode may be moved to any location within the pink area of the back cover.

- **Document Size:** The overall document size for this template is shown in the lower left corner. The final cover PDF submitted must match this size.

**Pink and blue boxes must be completely covered when cover is submitted.**

1. In IngramSpark, create an account and set-up a password or Login.
2. Click on the Resources menu across the top and choose Tools.
3. You should be viewing the Self-Publishing Tools page now. Scroll down past the three Calculator tools. You will find a Cover Template Generator button. Click on the button.
4. Another page appears. Fill in the information about your new book. If you don't understand something, click on the ? button for help. Duotone refers to the inside cover, which is usually blank.

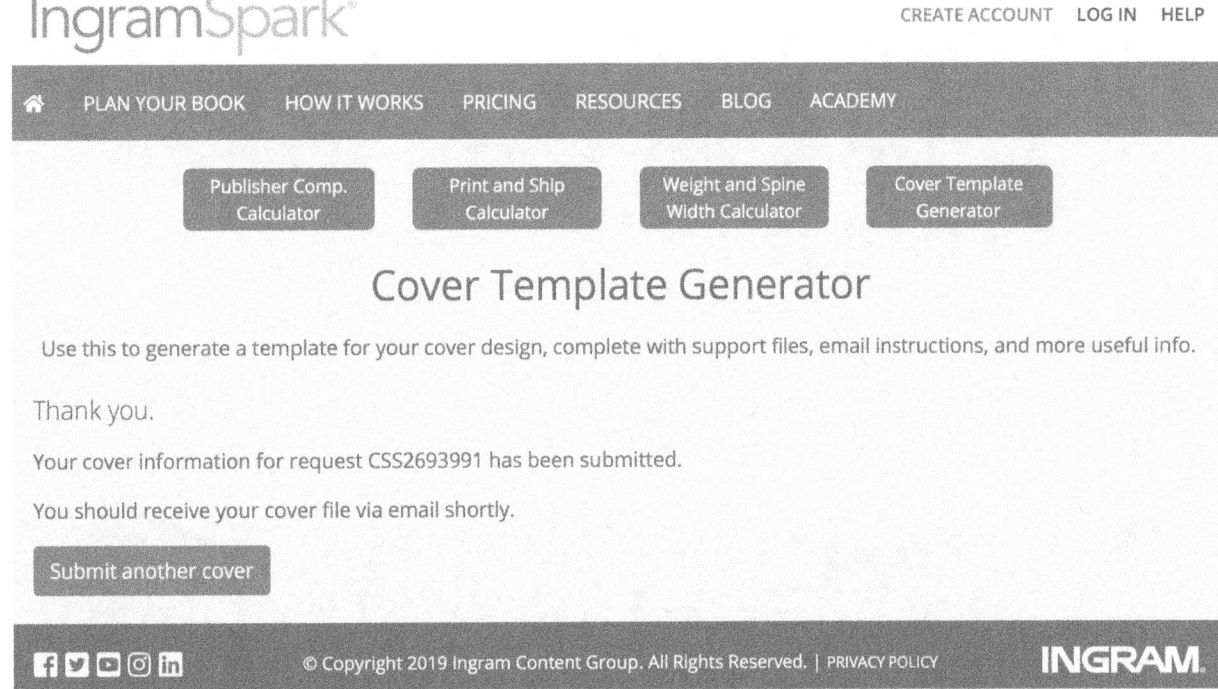

*Barbara A. Fanson*

CREATE ACCOUNT   LOG IN   HELP

PLAN YOUR BOOK   HOW IT WORKS   PRICING   RESOURCES   BLOG   ACADEMY

Publisher Comp. Calculator | Print and Ship Calculator | Weight and Spine Width Calculator | Cover Template Generator

# Cover Template Generator

Use this to generate a template for your cover design, complete with support files, email instructions, and more useful info.

Once you complete and submit the data below, we will email you back a template and support files to be used to build your cover.

Included in the email will be instructions for using the template, creating an appropriate PostScript file and distilling a PDF to our specifications.

* 13 Digit ISBN: 978-1-989361-11-5

Publisher Reference Number: 9111981

* Trim Size: 8.500" x 11.000" (280mm x 216mm)

Interior Color and Paper: ● Black & White
  ● White   B&W: printed on 50lb White paper
  ○ Color

Binding Type: ● Paperback
  ● Perfect Bound   Glued spine with color laminated cover
  ○ Saddle Stitch   Stapled pages with color laminated cover, 4-48 page count
  ○ Hardback

Laminate Type: ○ Gloss
  ● Matte

Duplex Cover: ○ Yes ● No

* Page Count: 60
(Multiple of 2, between 18 and 1200)

* File Type: PDF

* Email Address: learn@sterlinged.com

* Confirm Email Address: learn@sterlinged.com

## Optional Information

Price: 14.99

Currency: US Dollars

Price in Bar Code: Yes

Submit

© Copyright 2019 Ingram Content Group. All Rights Reserved.  |  PRIVACY POLICY

INGRAM

5. When you've completed the form, click on the Submit button.
6. Another window informs you that a PDF will be emailed to you.

## Working with the Cover Template

If you received a cover template from IngramSpark's Cover Generator, it will be a PDF with light blue and pink boxes. You can open it in Adobe Illustrator, or Adobe Photoshop. You can Place it into an Adobe InDesign document.

### Open Cover Template in Adobe Illustrator
1. Open it in Adobe Illustrator, select it and then choose Object > Clipping Mask > Release.
2. Choose Save As and save with a new name so your original template is preserved.
3. In the Layers Palette, lock the layer that the template is on and create a new layer for guidelines.
4. Drag guidelines from the ruler to the trim edge and ½" from trim so you know where the text should be—1/2" from the trim edge.
5. In the Layers Palette, add another layer for your artwork. Keep all your images and text on this layer.

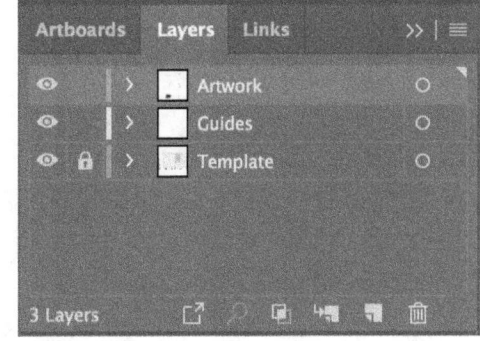

6. The barcode can be moved elsewhere on the back cover.
7. When you're finished creating the artwork for your back cover, front cover, and spine (if allowed), save this template as a PDF.

### Or, place Cover Template in Adobe InDesign
1. Create a new document in Adobe InDesign, which is 21" wide x 12" high.
2. Choose File > Place to import the cover template.
3. Choose File > Save As to save your new document.
4. In the Layers Palette, lock Layer 1 and rename it Template.
5. In the Layers Palette, create a new layer and name it Guidelines.
6. Drag guidelines from the ruler to the trim marks. Add guidelines 1/2" from the trim edge. Your type should not go beyond these guidelines.
7. In the Layers Palette, create a new layer and name it Artwork. Add your text and images to this layer.

8. The barcode can be moved elsewhere on the back cover.

The front cover covers the dark gray (light blue on the template). The photo goes past the trim marks at the top, right side, and bottom by 1/8" or 0.125".

## Add Back Cover

The barcode with ISBN and price can be moved anywhere on the back cover.

You have to have a barcode on the back cover, but you can also add a book description, quotation, author description, image, barcode, and optional QR code go on the back cover.

When you're thinking of buying a new book, what do you look at first? When potential buyers view your book, they usually look at the front cover first, turn the book over and look at the back cover. They are looking for the book description, which is either on the back cover, inside sleeve if the book has a dust cover, and inside the book. Sometimes, they read the first page or introduction to determine if they want to buy a book.

It might be helpful to have the color from the back cover continue onto the spine.

### Add a QR Code

A QR Code can be scanned with an App on your mobile device. It can lead viewers to your website or email address.

There are free QR Code Generators that you can find on the Internet. Some are free for a short time only, so you may wish to pay for it. http://www.barcode-generator.org

### Add Spine Text

If you have more than 48 pages, IngramSpark allows you to add text to the spine, but it must be in the pink area of the template; the type cannot touch the blue area.

If you have a 60-page book, the spine text will be 7 pt. very small type.

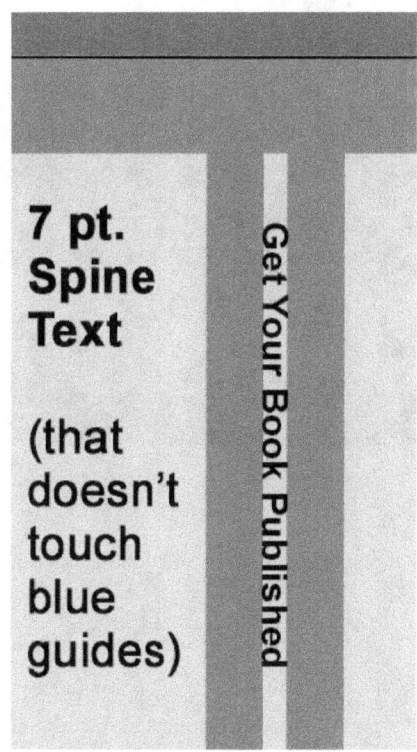

Figure 4: Enlarged Spine Text

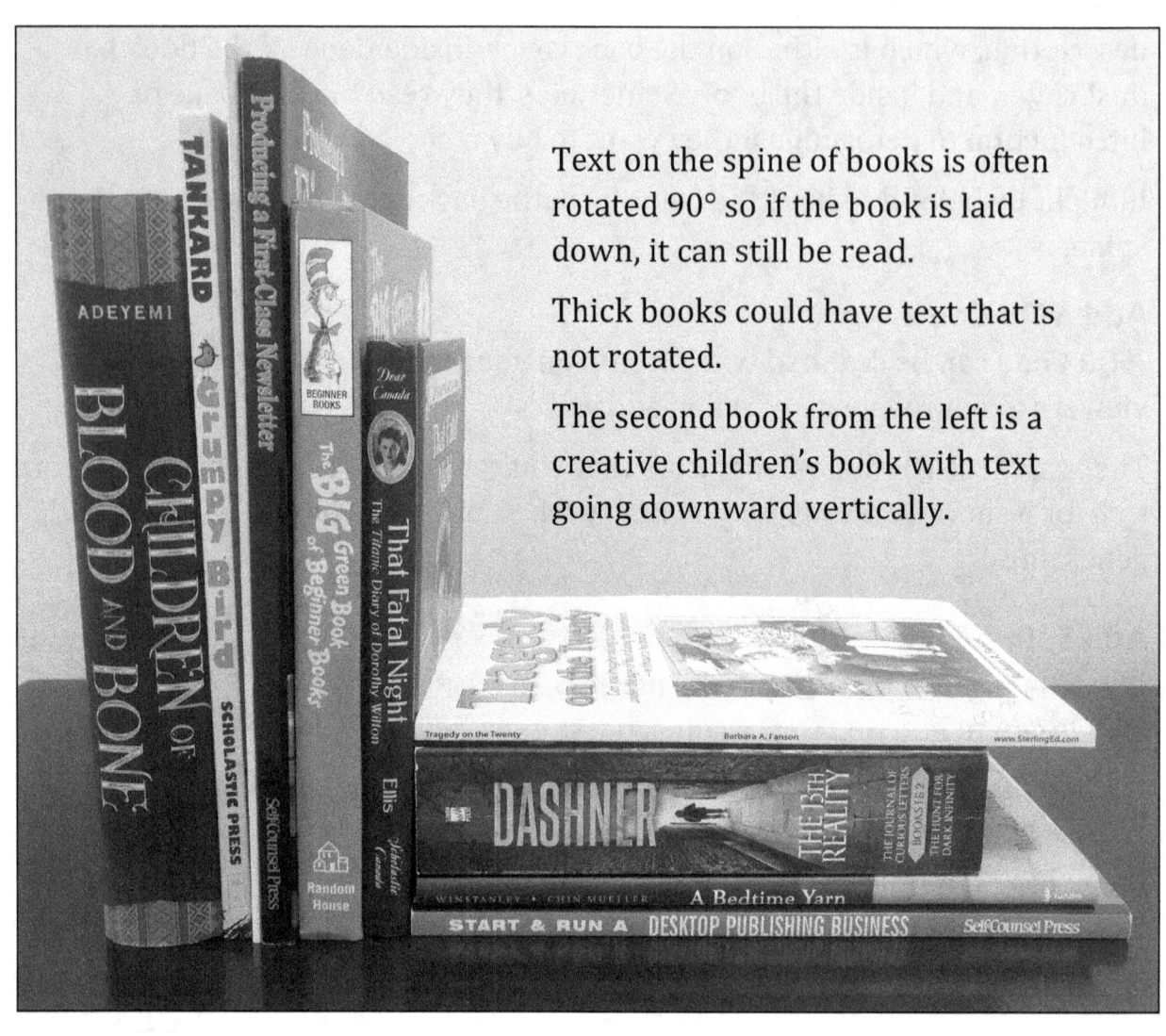

Text on the spine of books is often rotated 90° so if the book is laid down, it can still be read.

Thick books could have text that is not rotated.

The second book from the left is a creative children's book with text going downward vertically.

Some businesses are now using books like a business card. Other people want to print copies of their genealogical research. Maybe you want to share family recipes. Or you have an idea for a seminar that other people will find interesting. Do you have a story that beckons to be printed?

*Get Your Book Published* focuses on producing your books—1 copy, 100 copies, or 5,000 copies.

Barbara Fanson is an author and graphic designer. She has had 2 books published by Self-Counsel Press, a traditional book publisher, and has self-published over 30 books. She has written and illustrated 2 children's picture books, a historical fiction book, 2 non-fiction photographic books, a baby record book, and 20 software instruction manuals.

R = Red
G = Green
B = Blue

C = Cyan
M = Magenta
Y = Yellow
K = Black

ISBN 978-1-989361-11-5
51499

8.50 x 11.00
280 mm x 216 mm

## Case Laminate Books

With some print-on-demand book printers like IngramSpark, you can choose hardcover, softcover, or case laminate. A case laminate book has the cover printed on slightly larger stock and wrapped around and glued to the inside of the book. Therefore, the artwork will be slightly larger.

## Duplex Inside Cover

If you do not supply artwork for a Duplex Cover, your book will be printed with a white, inside cover. If you wish, you can pay a little more and have a pattern—or Duotone—printed on the inside cover. You can have the pattern printed on the first page, too. Plan to pay about 0.25¢ extra per book.

## Dust Jacket

The dust jacket is sometimes called a book jacket, dust wrapper, or dust cover. It is the detachable outer cover, usually made of paper and printed with text and images. It has two folded flaps to hold it to the book. The dust jacket protects the book covers from damage.

Classic books are worth more if their dust jacket is intact.

You can also have a dust jacket printed for hardcover books. A dust jacket is the loose sheet of paper that has flaps folded inside the book. Each flap is usually 3.125" in width. Often, the left flap has a book description, while the right flap has About the Author and Illustrator.

## Print Cost Comparison

Compare the cost of printing the same small paperback book with 200 pages on four different kinds of paper; three have color images, one has black.

| Black and White Interior Pages | $3.58 US |
| --- | --- |
| Standard Color 50 Interior Pages | $5.94 US |
| Standard Color 70 Interior Pages | $7.44 US |
| Premium Color Interior Pages | $14.64 US |

IngramSpark reserves the right to adjust prices. These are 2018 prices.

## Use Amazon KDP's Cover Creator

You can generate a cover using Amazon's KDP tool, but you cannot export it. The online file will be used for your book on Amazon only. You can customize the cover with a variety of layouts and fonts. Cover Creator uses the information you set up on their website and adds the book's ISBN to the barcode on the back cover. You can choose an image from their image gallery or upload your image. The Cover Creator tool accepts JPG, PNG, and GIF files.

Cover Creator is a free tool to help you design a basic cover that meets KDP specifications. If you're not happy with the free tool, you can check out KDP's do-it-yourself guidelines for designing a book cover and their templates. Or hire a professional designer so that you have images of the front cover to use in promotions.

1. Launch Cover Creator tool.
   To use the Cover Creator tool, you have to set up a book first on your Bookshelf. On the Content page for your book, scroll down to the Cover section and click on Launch Cover Creator.
2. Choose a design.
   Upload your photo for the cover or use KDP's stock images. Make sure your photo has a resolution of 300 ppi and CMYK color mode.
3. Customize the look.
   Choose a layout, color scheme, and font for your cover. Make sure your text is legible. The cover text should be large and clear.
4. Preview your cover design.
   Preview your cover to see how it will look when printed. Make sure the title text and author's name match the book details you entered. If you're not happy with the cover, you can start over. When you're satisfied with the cover, click Save & Submit.

Spine text will be automatically added in Cover Creator if you have more than 100 pages.

# 10
# Designing the front matter

The front cover of your book will be uploaded as a separate file and is covered in much more length in a later chapter. This chapter focuses on the front pages of your book—before chapter 1—and how to create them.

This chapter takes you step-by-step through the process of laying out the front matter at the front of the book and includes the first two pages of chapter 1. It was designed for an 8½" x 11" book, but you change the book size. Or, download this free Word book template:

www.SterlingEd.com/BookTemplate.html

Before you start to design your book, you should create a folder on your computer to save your story, photographs, artwork, and images in.

The front matter or preliminary pages is the first section of a book and is usually the smallest section in terms of the number of pages. The pages are numbered in lower-case Roman numerals, such as i, ii, iii, iv, v, vii, etc. Although each page is counted, they may not have a printed page number. Again, look at several books to see if they show the page numbers on the front pages.

The front matter of your book could have 20 pages but you should have a minimum of 3 pages, including a Title page, Copyright page, and Contents page. Refer to the chart called **Front matter pages and their purpose** on the next page.

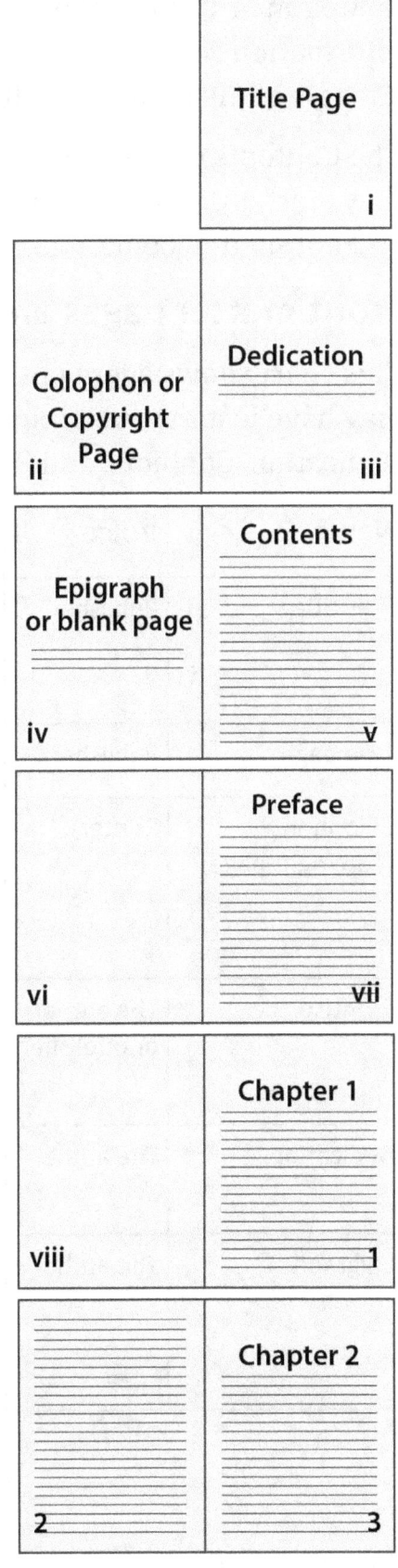

*Barbara A. Fanson*

The book title and author's name are usually printed on the Title page. The Colophon or Copyright page is usually on the next page with technical information such as edition dates, copyrights, typefaces, and the name and address of the publisher. Often, the copyright page follows the Title page.

The Contents page usually lists the headlines of each chapter and the page they start on. Subheads could also be listed. Some books—especially technical and non-fiction books—may have a Table of Drawings or Worksheets.

## Front matter pages and their purpose

This chart shows every possible page in the front matter, though your book may have just the most important pages: Title page, Colophon or Copyright, Dedication, Contents, and Preface.

| Name | Voice | Purpose |
| --- | --- | --- |
| Half-title | Publisher | Usually a single line in Capital letters, before the title page, and only contains the title with blank verso (next page is blank). |
| Title page | Publisher | The title and author as printed on the cover and spine. |
| Colophon (Copyright page) | Printer | Technical information such as edition dates, copyrights, typefaces, and the name and address of the printer or publisher. In modern books, this page is usually printed on the back of the Title page. |
| Frontispiece | The author or publisher | A decorative illustration on the verso, the blank page facing the title page. It may be related to the book's subject, or be a portrait of the author. ©www.Fanson.com |
| Dedication | The author | The page in a book, which the author names the person or people for whom the book was written. |
| Epigraph | The author | A phrase, quotation, or poem. The epigraph may serve as a preface, as a summary, as a counter-example, or to link the work to a wider literary canon, either to invite comparison or to enlist a conventional context. |

| Contents | Publisher | This is a list of chapter headings, subheads, and their respective page numbers. This includes all the front matter pages after the Contents page, the body matter, and the back matter. Ideally one page, but sometimes a double-page spread. Non-fiction or technical books may include a list of figures and a list of tables. |
|---|---|---|
| Foreword | A real person, other than the author. | Often, a foreword will reveal the relationship between the writer of the foreword and the writer of the story. Sometimes, a foreword will appear in later editions of a book and explains how this new edition is different than previous editions. |
| Preface | The author | A Preface usually covers the story of how the book came into being, or how the idea for the book was developed. This is often followed by thanks and acknowledgments to people who were helpful to the author during the writing process.      ©www.Fanson.com |
| Acknowledgment | The author | Sometimes a part of the Preface, rather than a separate section, it acknowledges those who contributed to the creation of the book. |
| Introduction | The author | A beginning section that states the purpose and goals of the book. |
| Prologue | The narrator or a character in the book | A prologue is an opening to a story that establishes the setting and gives background information. Sometimes, it is an earlier story that ties into the main one and other miscellaneous information. |

# Designing the layout of a book

**If you see this spider, it must be fall**

The Yellow and Black Garden Spider is a large arachnid, which spins an orb or circular web.

The female spider is black with symmetrical patches of bright yellow. The legs are reddish brown at the base and change to black toward the tips. The male spider is much smaller and doesn't have the bold colors like females. The female is about three times larger than males.

Figure 5: Sometimes children's picture books will have the image on the right-hand page.

Book margins and bleeds were discussed in chapter 6. Now, how do you want your book to look? Will you have chapters? Will each chapter start on a new page? Some books start a new chapter on a right-hand page. Will you have extra space above the chapter head?

Some novels usually don't have subheads, which is okay when you have a smaller page size. But when you have a bigger page size like 8.5"x11", it's better to break up all the grey text with some black, bold subheads.

---

You can have extra space between paragraphs to separate paragraphs. Extra space adds to the readability of the text.

Subheads and bulleted text help to break up the grey text and add a graphic element to the text—even without images!

**Subhead**

The female spider is black with symmetrical patches of bright yellow. The legs are reddish brown at the base and black toward the tips.

- Spiders are arachnids
- Female is 3 times larger than male
- Female is more colorful than male
- Female spins orb or circular web
- The female may eat the male after mating

If you see the Yellow and Black Garden Spider, then fall is coming.

---

A first paragraph after a head or subhead may not be indented.

But, you may wish to indent all new paragraphs after the first paragraph.

The Yellow and Black Garden Spider is a large arachnids which spin a orb, circular web.

The female spider is black with symmetrical patches of bright yellow. The legs are reddish brown at the base and change to black toward the tips. The male spider is much smaller and don't have the bold colors. The female is about three times larger than the males.

If you see the Yellow and Black Garden Spider, then fall is coming. The Yellow and Black Garden Spider is a large arachnids which spin a orb, circular web.

The female spider is black with symmetrical patches of bright yellow. The legs are reddish brown at the base and change to black toward the tips. The male spider is much smaller and don't have the bold colors. The female is about three times larger than the males.

---

Bullets and page numbers are also effective at providing "color" to an otherwise grey page. They also help to break up the monotony and reading style of the page.

How will you treat new paragraphs? Will you indent the first line to indicate a new paragraph or use extra space between paragraphs like this book?

Photographs, illustrations, charts, and tables add a graphic element to pages. They also illustrate important information or data.

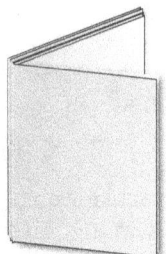

### Subhead

The female spider is black with symmetrical patches of bright yellow. The legs are reddish brown at the base and change to black toward the tips. The male spider is much smaller and doesn't have the bold colors like females. The female is about three times larger than the male.

- Spiders are arachnids
- Female is 3 times larger than male
- Female is more colorful than male
- Female spins orb or circular web
- The female may eat the male after mating

If you see the Yellow and Black Garden Spider, then fall is coming. The Yellow and Black Garden Spider is a large arachnid, which spins a orb or circular web.

The female spider is black with symmetrical patches of bright yellow. The legs are reddish brown at the base and change to black toward the tips. The male spider is much smaller and doesn't have the bold colors like females. Females are about three times larger than males.

If you see the Yellow and Black Garden Spider, then fall is coming. The Yellow and Black Garden Spider is a large arachnid, which spins an orb or circular web.

The female spider is black with symmetrical patches of bright yellow. The legs are reddish brown at the base and black toward the tips.

Photographs, illustrations, graphs, and tables are perfect for breaking up lots of text. They can also illustrate important information and data.

Some children's picture books have the photograph or illustration on the right-hand page, and the story on the left-hand page.

Children's books usually have larger type and are easy to read.

Some children's picture books have the image on the right-hand page and the story on the left side.

Some picture books will have full-page photographs or illustrations with the text printed on the image. Other books have images across the bottom and text at the top.

Sometimes, the text is placed in a feathered, white translucent box.

Sometimes, the text has to be changed to white so it is legible.

A graphic novel may have the page divided into several smaller images—either color or black and white.

Would your book benefit from illustrations or photographs?

This page has full-page, full-color images.

A graphic novel may have several smaller images.

This page has white margins around the edge. The text can be above or below the image.

This photo has a bleed—the photo goes past the edge and is trimmed off after printing. The text is at least 1/2" from the edge.

Textbooks may have two or three columns so the line length won't be so long.

**Textbooks may have 2 columns of text**

The Yellow and Black Garden Spider is a large arachnid, which spins an orb or circular web.

The female spider is black with symmetrical patches of bright yellow. The legs are

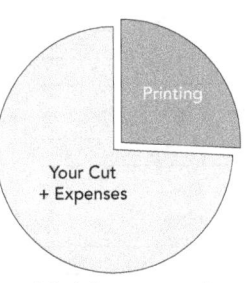

reddish brown at the base and change to black toward the tips. The male spider is much smaller and doesn't have the bold colors like females. The female is about three times larger than males.

The female spider is black with symmetrical patches of bright yellow.

**Images can be 1 column wide or 2**

Yellow and Black Garden Spiders are large arachnid, which spins an orb web.

The female spider is black with symmetrical patches of bright yellow.

The legs are reddish brown at the base and change to black toward the tips. The male spider visits.

The images, photographs, graphs, and tables can be one column wide, two columns wide, or three columns.

20  Title of the Book

Author's Name or Chapter  21

New Chapter Headline

## Headers and Footers

A header is the type across the top of a page. A footer is the type at the bottom of a page. All printed books should have a page number. Ebooks do not have to have a page number since the

Barbara A. Fanson

61

electronic device will number the screen.

If you're writing a novel, look at several novels. Are there headers, footers, or both? Where is the page number? If you're writing a children's picture book, look at other picture books. If you're writing a non-fiction book, look at similar books.

What should you include in the header or footer? Sometimes the page number is on the outside edge—the top-left corner of left pages and the top-right corner of right pages. But some novels have the page number centered at the bottom in the footer and no type in the header. Other novels have the page number centered at the bottom, the author's name in the left header, and the book title in the right header.

Often the font used for the headers and footers is different from the font of the story text so that it doesn't confuse readers. Sometimes the font for headers and footers was italic, but sometimes, the page numbers were creative.

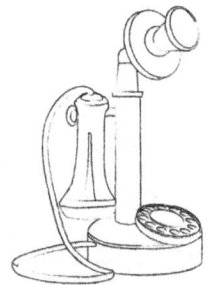

*Tragedy on the Twenty* (above) is a historical fiction book. Because dates were important to the story, it is shown above the chapter head, which is on the right page. The left page is the end of the previous chapter, so author Barbara Fanson chose to draw a picture to illustrate something from that time period. Candlestick telephones were starting to come into people's homes.

Notice the page numbers are on the outside edge. The graphic designer chose to have a rule separating the story text and the footer because previous instructional books by the same author had a rule. Notice that all new paragraphs are indented and there is more space between paragraphs.

*Tragedy on the Twenty* (above) has justified type—the text is aligned on both sides like most novels, but the headline is centered.

# 11
# Preparing a book for print

## Saving your book as a PDF

You may need to save your document as a PDF (Portable Document Format) so that other people can read it. How should you send save it?

### Save a PDF in Microsoft Word

In Microsoft Word, do not choose File > Save As to save it as a PDF. Instead, choose File > Print, a dialog box appears.

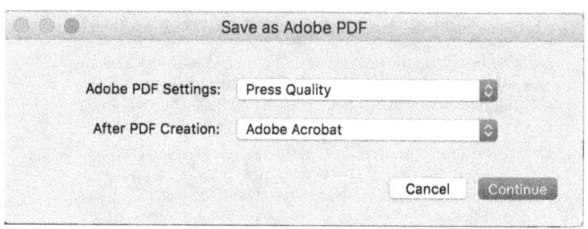

Click on PDF and choose Adobe PDF. A small dialog box appears.

For files to be printed, change Adobe PDF Settings to Press Quality.

Change After PDF Creation to Adobe Acrobat Pro.

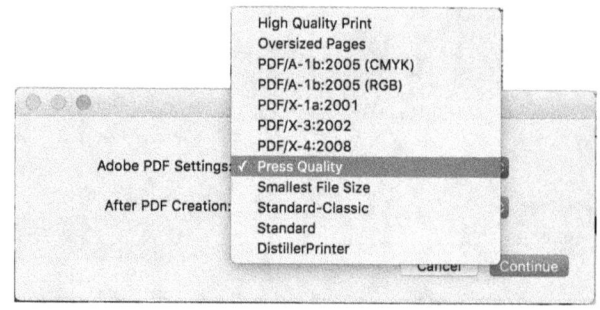

Click Continue. Save your document. Your file will open in Adobe Acrobat.

### Single or double-page

Sometimes, it is easier to read a single-page PDF than a double page. Online printers such as IngramSpark and KDP prefer single pages.

## Book Checklist for Covers

- ❏ To upload a book cover to IngramSpark, use their custom Cover Generator tool, located in the Tools section of their website. Just fill in the required fields and a custom template will be emailed to you.
- ❏ The cover file PDF should be a separate file from the interior pages.
- ❏ PDFs created by choosing Save As in MS Word are not supported, but you can create a PDF in the Print dialog box. (I would open the PDF in Adobe Acrobat and save again.)
- ❏ Barcodes are mandatory on all covers. 100% black only and placed on a white box or background.
- ❏ Resolution for images on front or back cover must be 300 ppi (pixels per inch). Use CMYK color (cyan, magenta, yellow, black).
- ❏ A bleed of 0.125" or 1/8" must be added to all 4 sides.
- ❏ Spine Type is allowed for 48 pages or more in IngramSpark, but must have space on all sides:
  Spines 0.35" and larger – 0.0625" or 2mm left/right sides
  Spines smaller than 0.35" – 0.03125" or 1mm left/right sides
- ❏ For text on the cover that is less than 24 pt., use 100% black only.
- ❏ All spot colors with or without transparencies must be converted to CMYK.
- ❏ Please make sure you are satisfied with your files before uploading. There may be a $25 charge for all revised file uploads after submission is complete.

**R = Red**
**G = Green**
**B = Blue**

**C = Cyan**
**M = Magenta**
**Y = Yellow**
**K = Black**

## Book Checklist for Interior Pages

This checklist will help you to avoid the most common causes of file rejection and delays. This list may not contain everything needed to create a print-on-demand file that will get approved.

- Interior file must be uploaded as a separate file from the cover.
- PDFs created by choosing Save As in MS Word are not supported.
- Use single-page format or 1-up page. Do not use double-page spreads.
- Do not include crop marks, registration marks, or printers' marks.
- All fonts must be embedded.
- Make sure the last page is blank.
- Margins must be at least .5" from the final trim size on all sides. This includes page numbers and non-bleeding text and art. If text or images are too close to the trim edges, they could be cut during printing and binding. A margin is white space around the edge of this page.
- A gutter margin with no ink of .125" is required on the binding side of interior pages. Any books with less than 48 pages can be saddle-stitched and do not require gutter margins.
- Color interior pages must have a bleed of at least .125" past final trim size, except on binding edge.
- Bleeds are not guaranteed on Black and white interior pages.
- For black and white interior pages, do not include spot colors and all images should be converted to grayscale.
- For color images on interior pages, photos should be CMYK (Cyan, Magenta, Yellow, Black) with a resolution of 72 ppi (pixels per inch) or higher.
- All spot colors with or without transparencies must be converted to CMYK.
- For revisions, the entire file must be re-uploaded; you cannot upload a few pages.

# What's the "key" to keywords?

If you publish a book online using websites like Amazon or IngramSpark, they will ask for keywords. What are the words that appear in your book often? Keywords define what your content is about. In terms of Search Engine Optimization, they're the words that searchers enter into search engines.

When saving a Microsoft Word document, a second box comes up asking for title and keywords. Do you take the time to fill in the keywords? If you did fill in the keywords, it would be easier to search for these types of keywords.

## Understanding Title Metadata

Metadata is the key to standing out in a crowded book market. Metadata is working in the background to get your book found. If set up properly, you can grab the attention of more readers and achieve your highest sales potential. For example, if I search Amazon's website to find book baby record books, how many books do you think will appear? 20 pages of 16 listings per page! That's 320 baby record books!

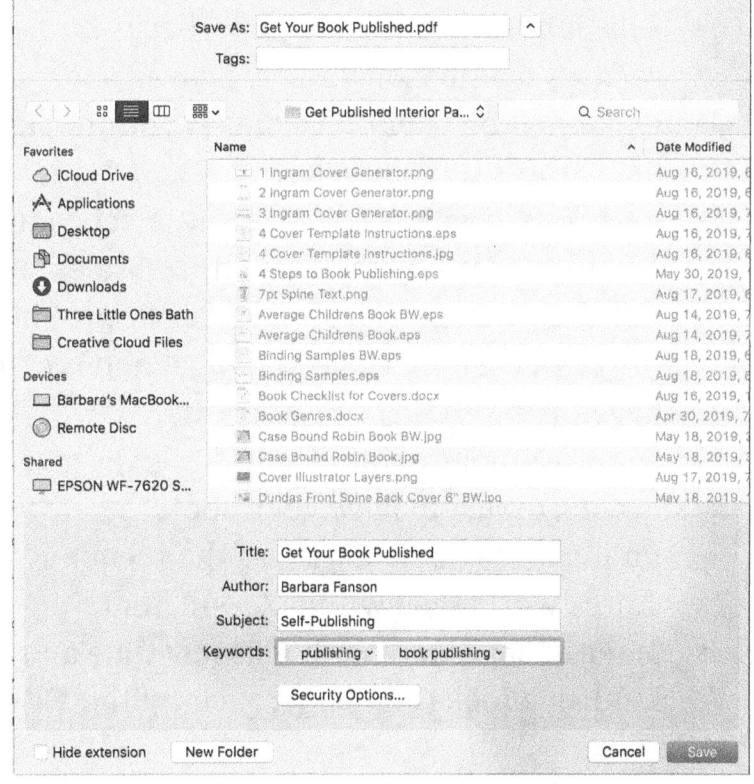

If people want to find your book, they can Google or search Amazon by the book title or author's name. If it's a book about robins, then robin would be a keyword. Choose at least seven keywords for your book.

To save a Microsoft Word document as a PDF for printing, do **not** go to File > Save As. Instead:

- Choose File > Print. The Print dialog box appears. Click on the PDF button in the bottom-left corner. A box appears.
- Name your PDF and add some keywords to aid in searching for this file.

## Advantages to publishing with IngramSpark

- For more information, check their website: IngramSpark.com
- They print 7,000 book catalogues and email 29,000 PDF catalogues to libraries, booksellers, and retailers.
- They charge $49 to set up a print book and eBook.
- From print-on-demand books to eBook publishing, they get your book around the world in 4 steps: create an account, upload your book, share with the world, and earn cash on every sale.
- Print 1 book or 1,000 books—print only what you need.
- eBooks so your book can be read on all digital book readers.
- Stunning color for photo books, children's books, graphic novels, more.
- All book formats: hardcover, paperback, and eBook.
- Author resources for helping you self-publish your books.

## Advantages to publishing with Amazon KDP

- For more information, check their website: kdp.amazon.com
- Amazon, a leader in online sales, owns kindle Direct Publishing.
- Self-publish eBooks and paperbacks for free and reach millions of readers on Amazon. (no hardcover books)
- Expanded Distribution exposes your books to online retailers, bookstores, and libraries.
- Earn 70% royalty from sales in select countries with KDP Select, which means higher revenue, maximized sales, and expanded audiences.
- Use their Amazon Marketing Services to help get your books in front of the right customers. Set a budget and create targeted ads based on keywords, products, or interests.
- Order Author Copies of your book for giveaways, book signings, special events, or just to have your book.
- Publishing a book takes less than 5 minutes and appears on Kindle stores worldwide within 24–48 hours.
- Make changes to your books any time and set your price.
- Publish eBooks and paperbacks with KDP for free—no setup charge.

## Uploading your book to IngramSpark

After completing the Before You Upload Your Book Form in this book, you're ready to upload your finished book.

You should have two finished files: the interior pages saved as a PDF, and the finished cover with the front cover, back cover, and spine in one PDF file.

If your book will have black and white pages, then all your headlines and images should be black or grayscale. If you have color images, change them to black or grayscale.

In Microsoft Word, do not choose File > Save As to save your document as a PDF. Go to Print instead.

1. Go to IngramSpark's website: www.IngramSpark.com. Either create an account or log in with your password.

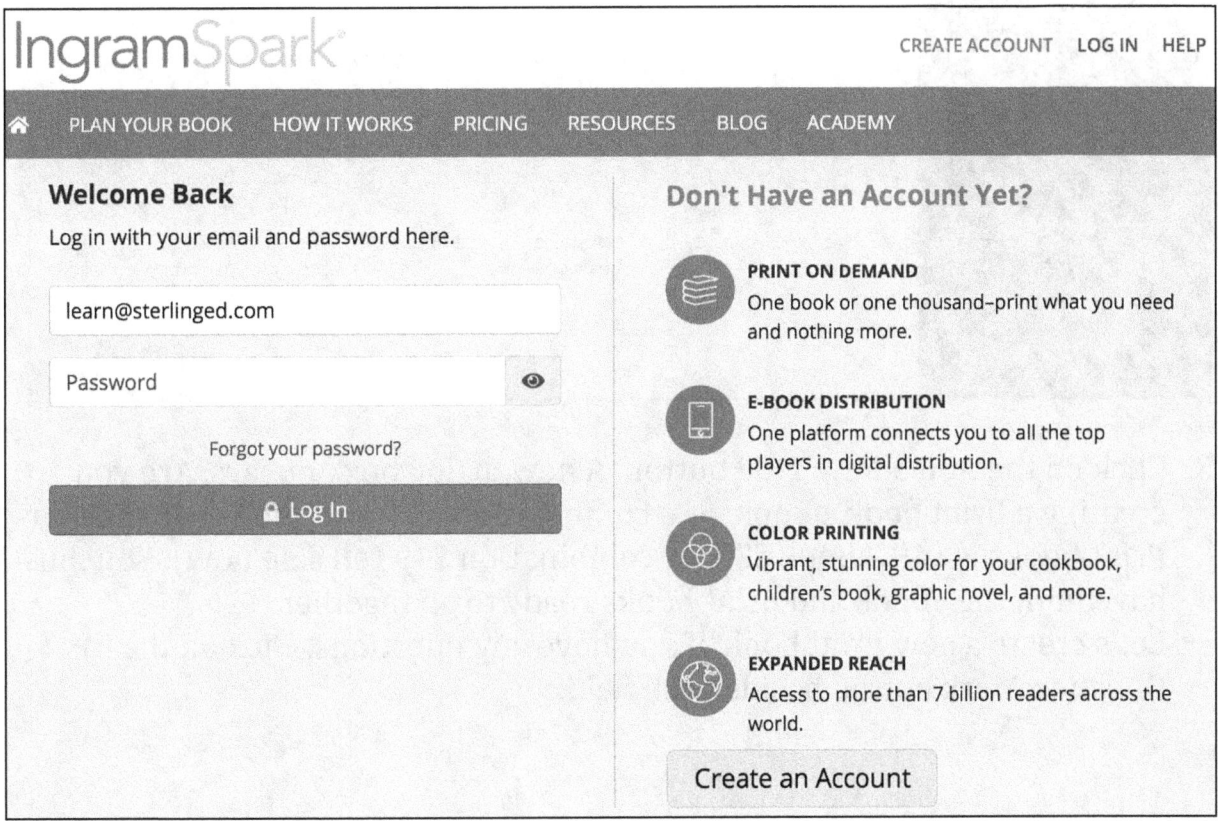

2. Once you log in, you will see your Dashboard with all your books.

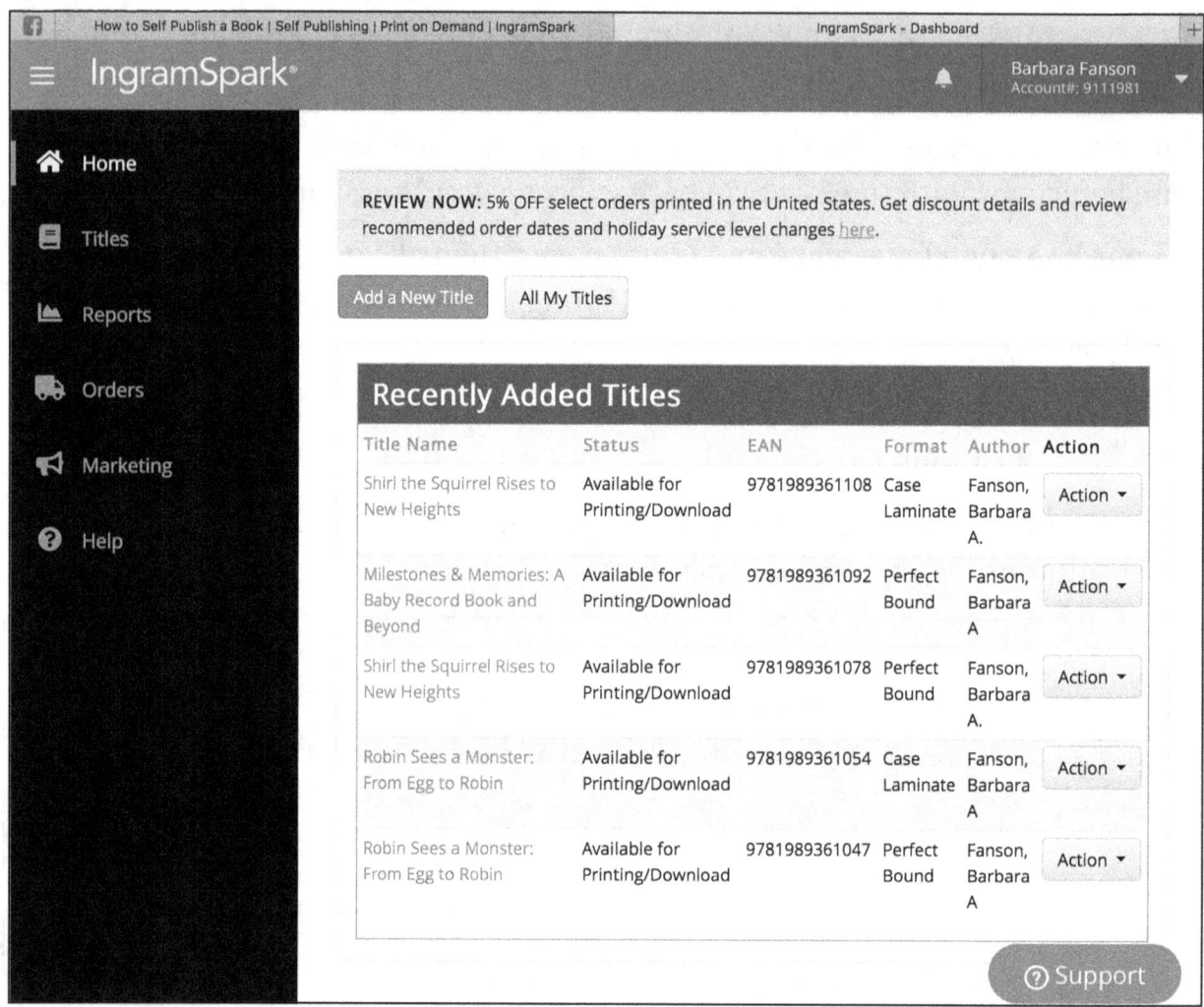

3. Click on the Add a New Title button. A new dialog box appears. Are you creating a Print book, eBook, or a combination of both? The Set-Up Fee for Print books is $49, eBook $25, or combination $49 (on sale now). You must have both the eBook and print books ready to go together.
Let's create a new print book. If you have any questions, click on the Question Mark button beside each field.

4. Complete the form and then click on the Continue to Step 2 of 5 button.

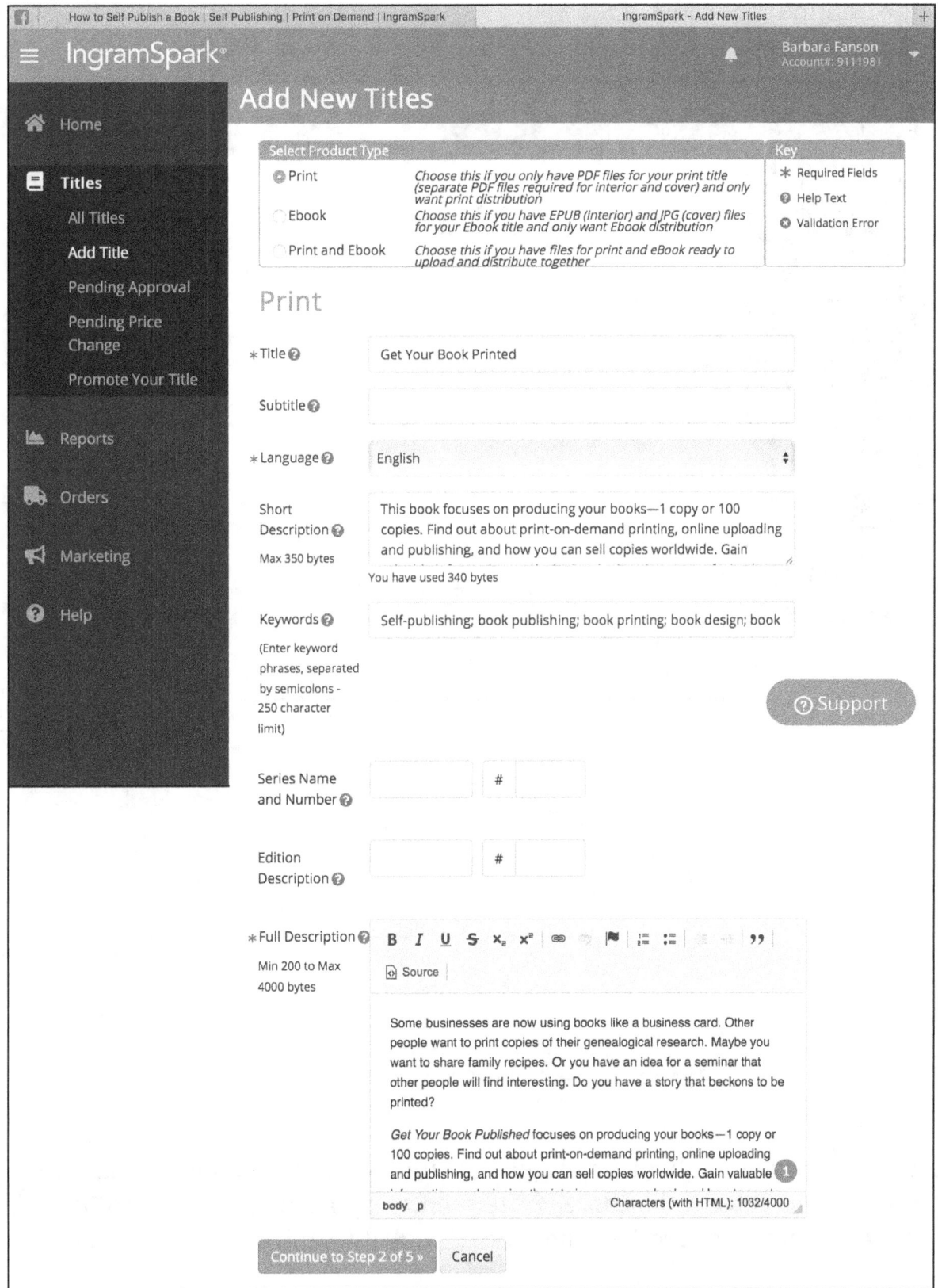

5. Fill in the information about the Author and Contributors. Then, click on the Continue to Step 3 of 5.
   You can stop at any time and resume when you log in again.

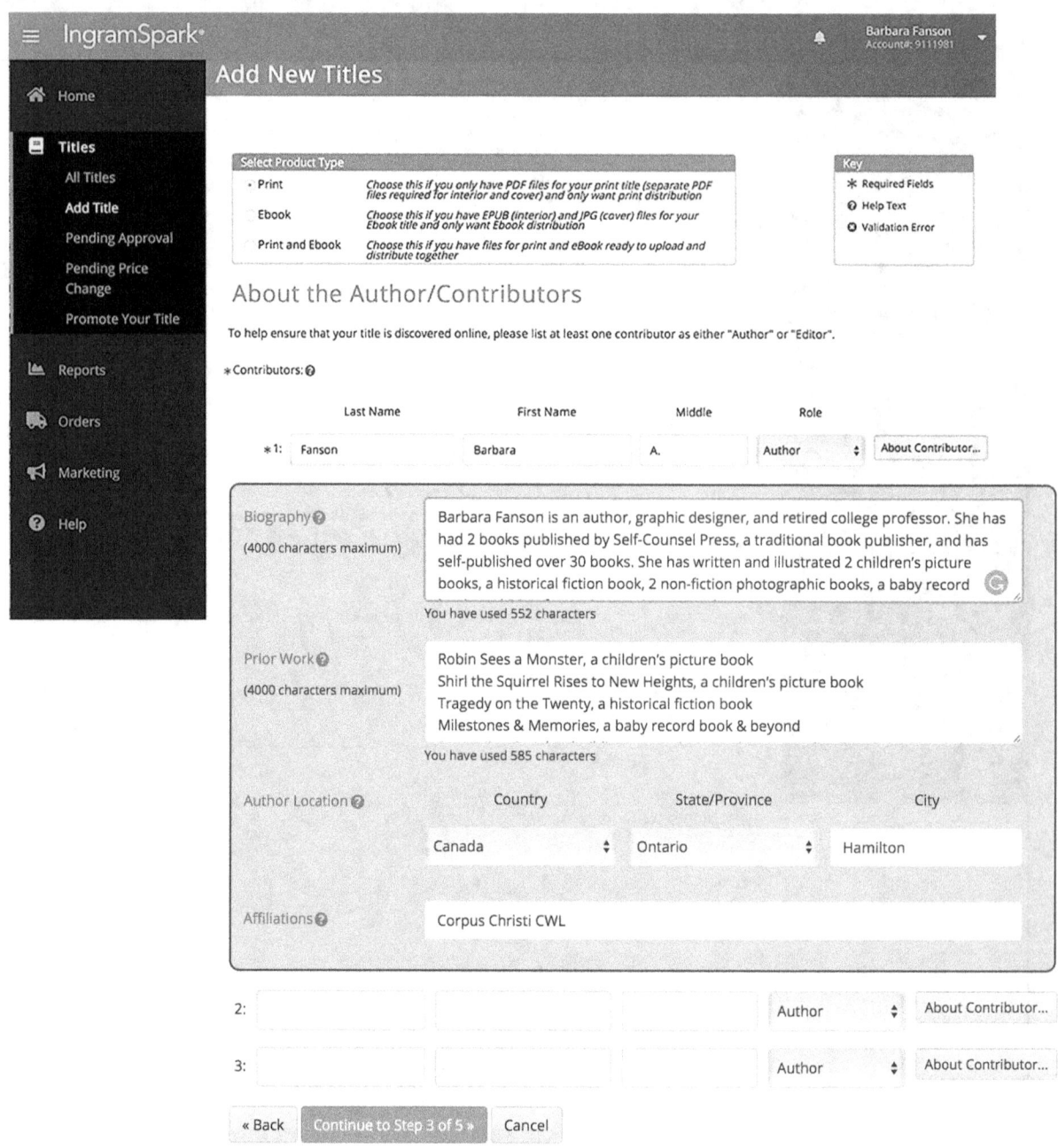

6. Where would your book be placed in a library? In the Subjects area, click on the Find Subjects button. Another window pops up. Type a word into the text field that describes the type of book it is, and click on the Search button.

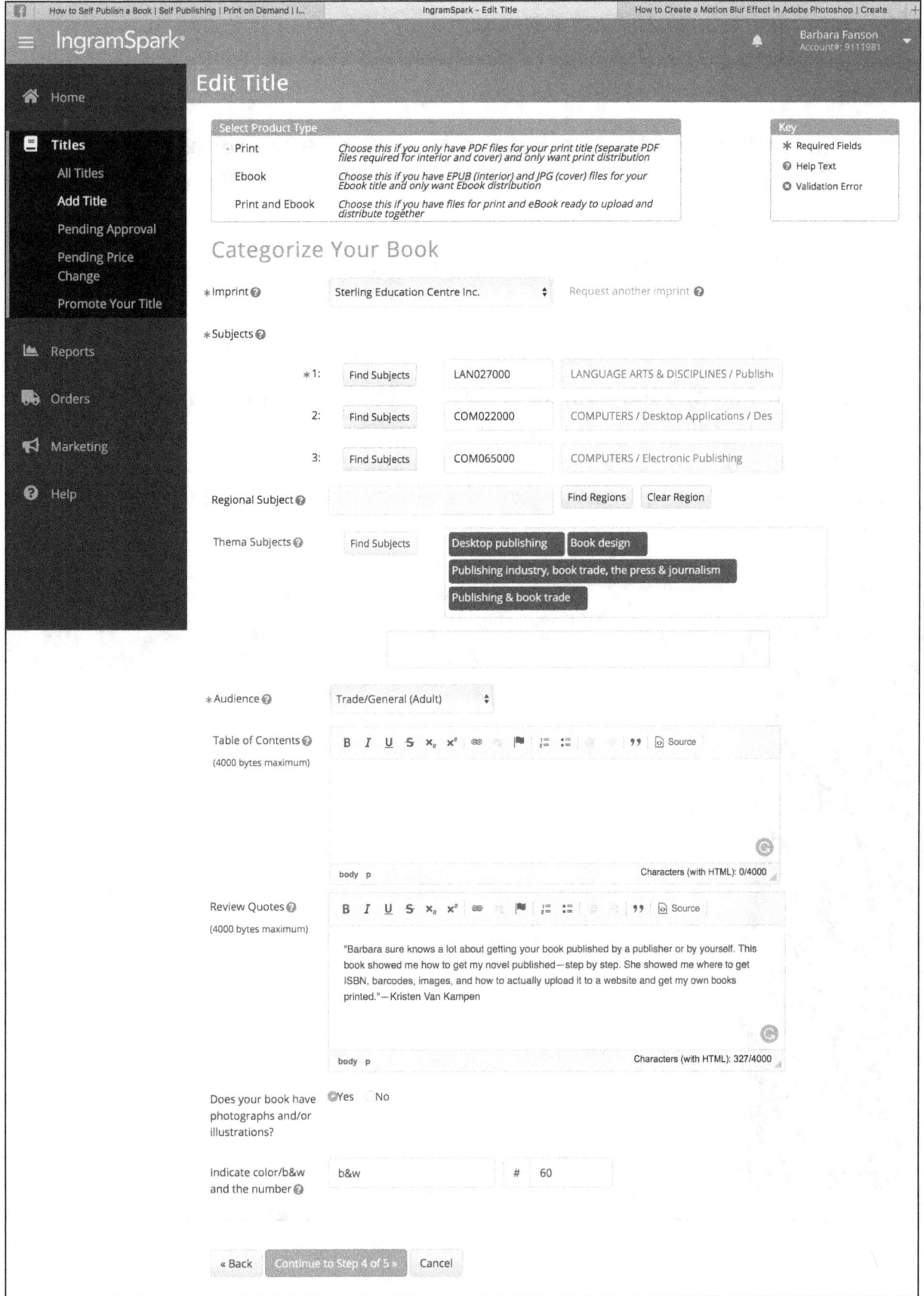

BISAC stands for Book Industry Standards and Communications. It is a list of standard subjects designed for the book trade in the U.S. and English-speaking Canada.

Choose at least one BISAC code, but three is better. BISAC codes help libraries and booksellers shelve books, categorize, market, and merchandise books. Choose codes that mirror the broadness of the content.

The first code you choose should be the most accurate and most specific code possible.

Avoid selecting codes that only represent one chapter or theme of the work.

7. When I clicked on Find Subjects button, I typed publishing and three choices appeared. I can choose one and repeat. You must have at least one BISAC code, but you can have up to three choices. When you click on a checkbox, the pop-up window will disappear and it will fill in the text field for you.

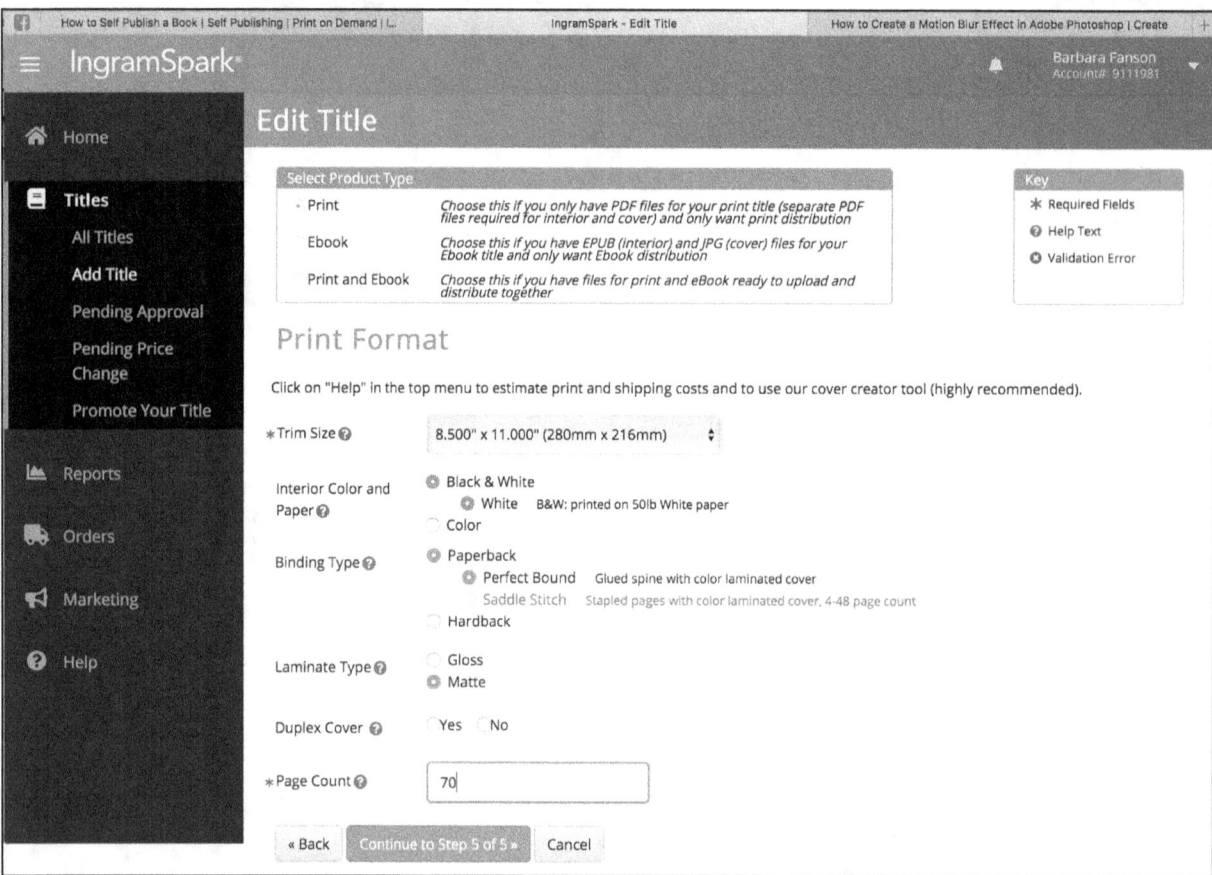

8. For Thema Subjects, click on the Find Subjects button. Another window pops up. If you know what category your book falls into, click on the left to expand it and click on the one that most fits your book.
   You can also click in the Criteria field, type a topic, and click on the Search button. You may choose several subject areas.
9. If you have a table of contents, you can paste it. Do you have any quotes or reviews from people? Post them. Click on the Continue button.
10. Are the interior pages of your book color or black & white? What kind of laminate finish do you want on the cover: gloss or matte?

## IngramSpark's book trim sizes

11. Trim Size is the finished size of your book after it has been printed, bound, and trimmed.

## Pricing your book

12. Pricing your book is probably the hardest decision you have to make. How much should you charge for your book?
    iBooks wants all electronic book prices to end in .99 cents.
    Establish a U.S. price for your book before converting to other currencies.
    I have listed some popular book prices on the next few pages.
    Or use their Currency Converter tool to convert the U.S. book price to other popular currencies.
13. How much of a discount are you willing to provide to booksellers and libraries? They will sell the book at the price you set, but they buy it at a discount to help pay their expenses.
    55% trade (retailer preference) or Other (between 30% and 54%)

```
4.000" x 6.000" (152mm x 102 mm)
4.000" x 7.000" (178mm x 102 mm)
4.250" x 7.000" (178mm x 108 mm)
4.370" x 7.000" (178mm x 111mm)
4.720" x 7.480" (190mm x 120mm)
5.000" x 8.000" (203mm x 127mm)
5.000" x 7.000" (178mm x 127mm)
5.060" x 7.810" (198mm x 129mm)
5.250" x 8.000" (203mm x 133mm)
5.500" x 8.500" (216mm x 140mm)
5.500" x 8.250" (210mm x 140mm)
5.830" x 8.270" (210mm x 148mm) A5
6.000" x 9.000" (229mm x 152mm)
6.140" x 9.210" (234mm x 156mm)
6.500" x 6.500" (165mm x 165mm)
6.625" x 10.250" (260mm x 168mm)
6.690" x 9.610" (244mm x 170mm)
7.000" x 10.000" (254mm x 178mm)
7.440" x 9.690" (246mm x 189mm)
7.500" x 9.250" (235mm x 191mm)
8.000" x 8.000" (203mm x 203mm)
8.000" x 10.000" (254mm x 203mm)
8.000" x 10.880" (276mm x 203mm)
8.250" x 11.000" (280mm x 210mm)
8.250" x 10.750" (273mm x 210 mm)
8.268" x 11.693" (297mm x 210mm) A4
8.500" x 9.000" (229mm x 216mm)
8.500" x 8.500" (216mm x 216mm)
✓ 8.500" x 11.000" (280mm x 216mm)
11.000" x 8.500" (216mm x 280mm)
```

14. If the customer does not like the quality of the book, can they return it? No, Yes – Deliver, or Yes – Destroy.

# Converting currency for book prices

*Based on rate of 1.29220 on March 5, 2019.*

*©2019 Sterling Education Centre Inc.*

| U.S. | GBP | Euros | Canadian | Australia |
|------|-----|-------|----------|-----------|
| 2.99 | 2.26880303 | 2.64446364 | 3.863678 | 4.2190395 |
| 4.99 | 3.78639703 | 4.41333564 | 6.448078 | 7.0411395 |
| 6.99 | 5.30399103 | 6.18220764 | 9.032478 | 9.8632395 |
| 8.99 | 6.82158503 | 7.95107964 | 11.616878 | 12.6853395 |
| 9.99 | 7.58038203 | 8.83551564 | 12.909078 | 14.0963895 |
| 12.99 | 9.85677303 | 11.48882364 | 16.785678 | 18.3295395 |
| 14.99 | 11.37436703 | 13.25769564 | 19.370078 | 21.1516395 |
| 19.99 | 15.16835203 | 17.67987564 | 25.831078 | 28.2068895 |
| 24.99 | 18.96233703 | 22.10205564 | 32.292078 | 35.2621395 |

*Remember that iBooks wants all prices to end in .99 cents.*

15. The last page is for uploading the file for your interior pages and the file for your cover. Once you click OK, you will have to wait for your file to be reviewed. IngramSpark will email you a PDF of the book for you to check over. Make sure you are satisfied with your files before you upload them because it may cost you to revise a file.

> Your On Sale Date 9-10-2019 is in the future. Orders placed for this title will be held and released prior to this date to receive product on or before the On Sale date provided. The publisher has the option to print and ship an order prior to the On Sale date and will have the option to release the hold in the ordering screen. For additional information select the On Sale Date help text. Do you still want to save?
>
> Cancel   OK

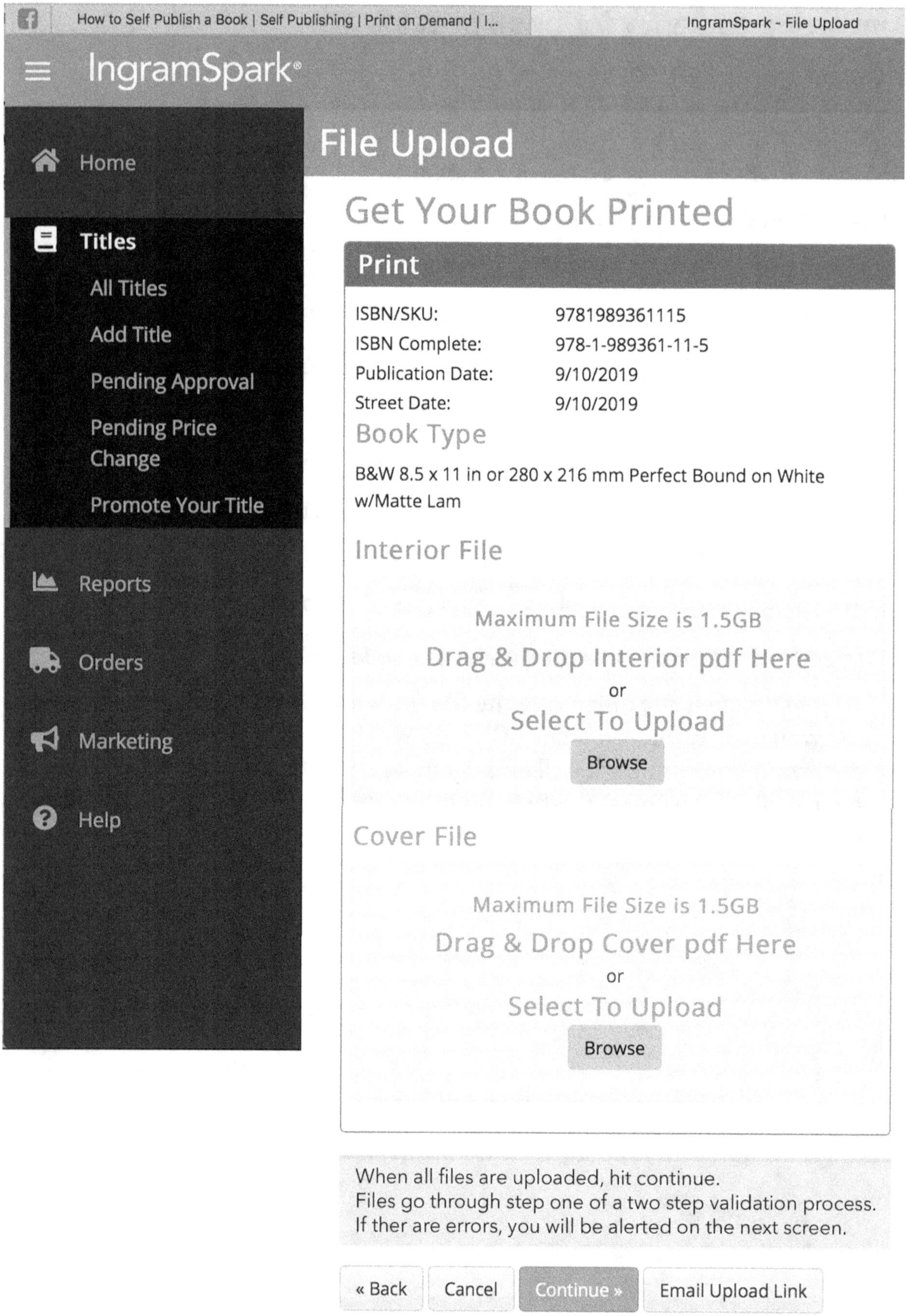

How to Self Publish a Book | Self Publishing | Print on Demand | I...
IngramSpark - File Upload
IngramSpark
Home
Titles
All Titles
Add Title
Pending Approval
Pending Price Change
Promote Your Title
Reports
Orders
Marketing
Help
File Upload
Get Your Book Printed
Print
ISBN/SKU: 9781989361115
ISBN Complete: 978-1-989361-11-5
Publication Date: 9/10/2019
Street Date: 9/10/2019
Book Type
B&W 8.5 x 11 in or 280 x 216 mm Perfect Bound on White w/Matte Lam
Interior File
Maximum File Size is 1.5GB
Drag & Drop Interior pdf Here
or
Select To Upload
Browse
Cover File
Maximum File Size is 1.5GB
Drag & Drop Cover pdf Here
or
Select To Upload
Browse
When all files are uploaded, hit continue.
Files go through step one of a two step validation process.
If ther are errors, you will be alerted on the next screen.
« Back
Cancel
Continue »
Email Upload Link

## Uploading your book to Amazon

CreateSpace has been changed to KDP.Amazon.com. After completing the Before You Upload Your Book Form in this book, you're ready to upload your finished book.

You should have two finished files: the interior pages which can be a Microsoft Word file or PDF, and the finished cover with the front cover, back cover, and spine in one PDF file.

If your book will have black and white pages, then all your headlines and images should be black or grayscale. If you have color images in Microsoft Word, make sure to convert them to grayscale.

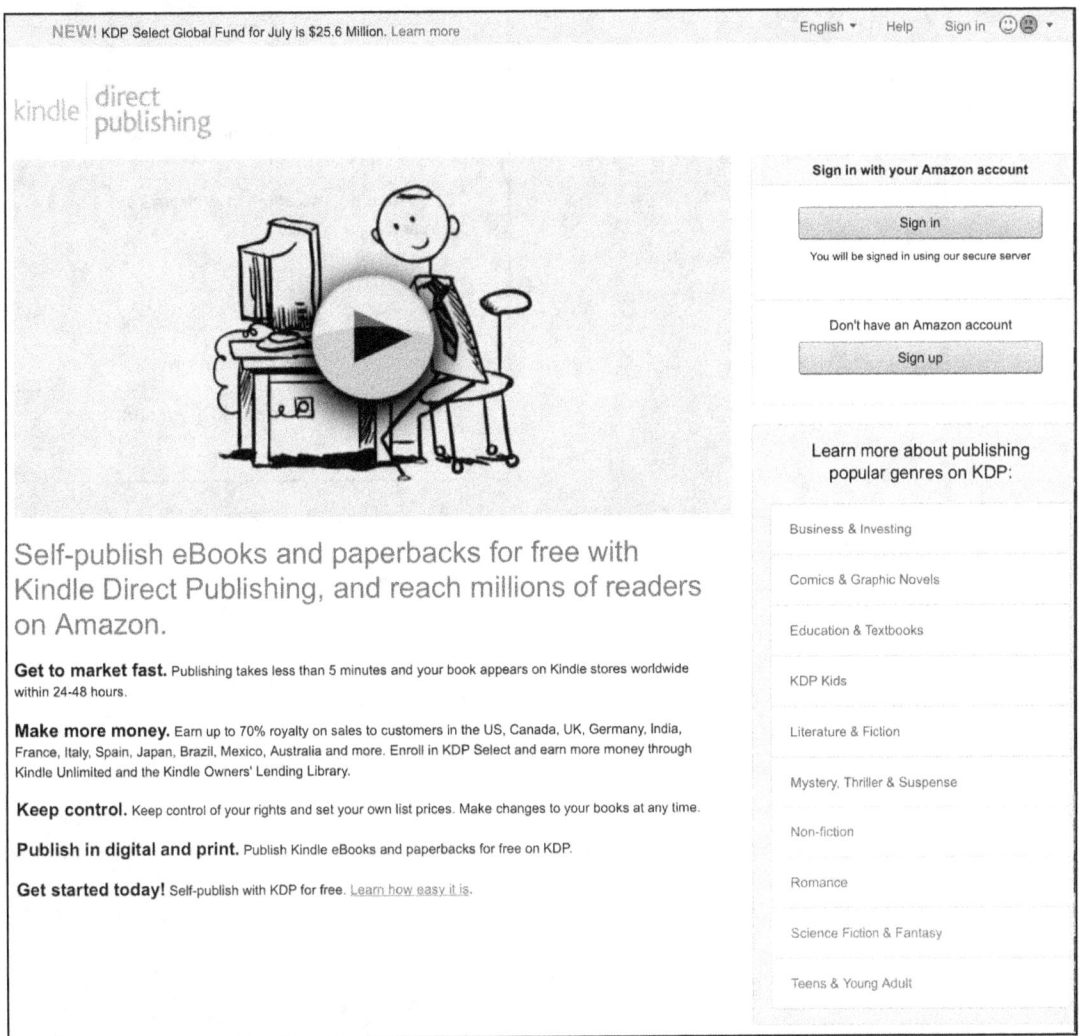

1. Go to Amazon's website: KDP.Amazon.com and Sign In or Sign Up.

2. A second window will appear requesting your password or sign up.
3. The next window shows all your books. The eBooks are automatically created. You can Promote and Advertise existing books, Order Author Copies, or Continue Setup of books that have not been completed.

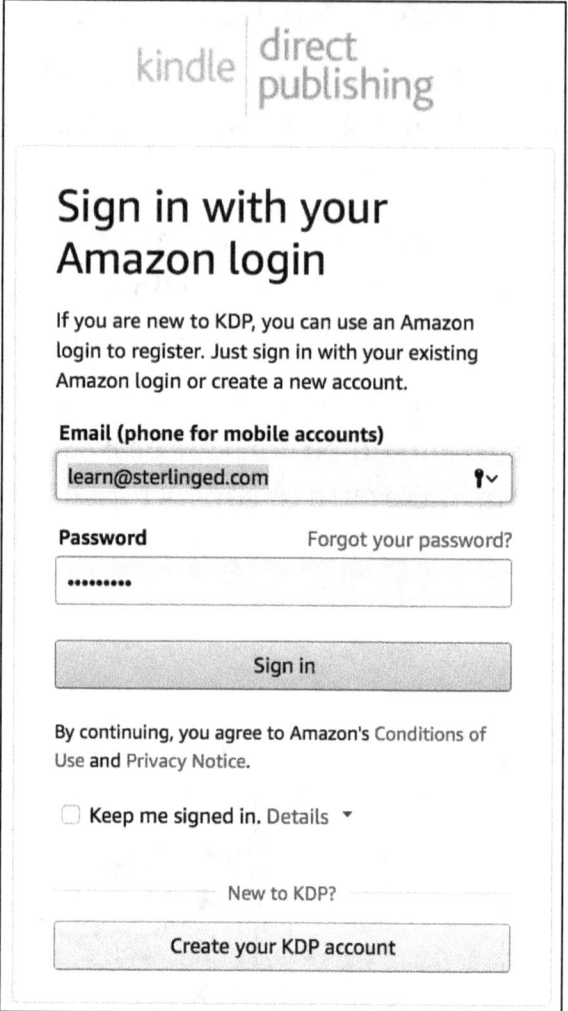

4. To create a new book, click on Paperback in the Create New Title section.

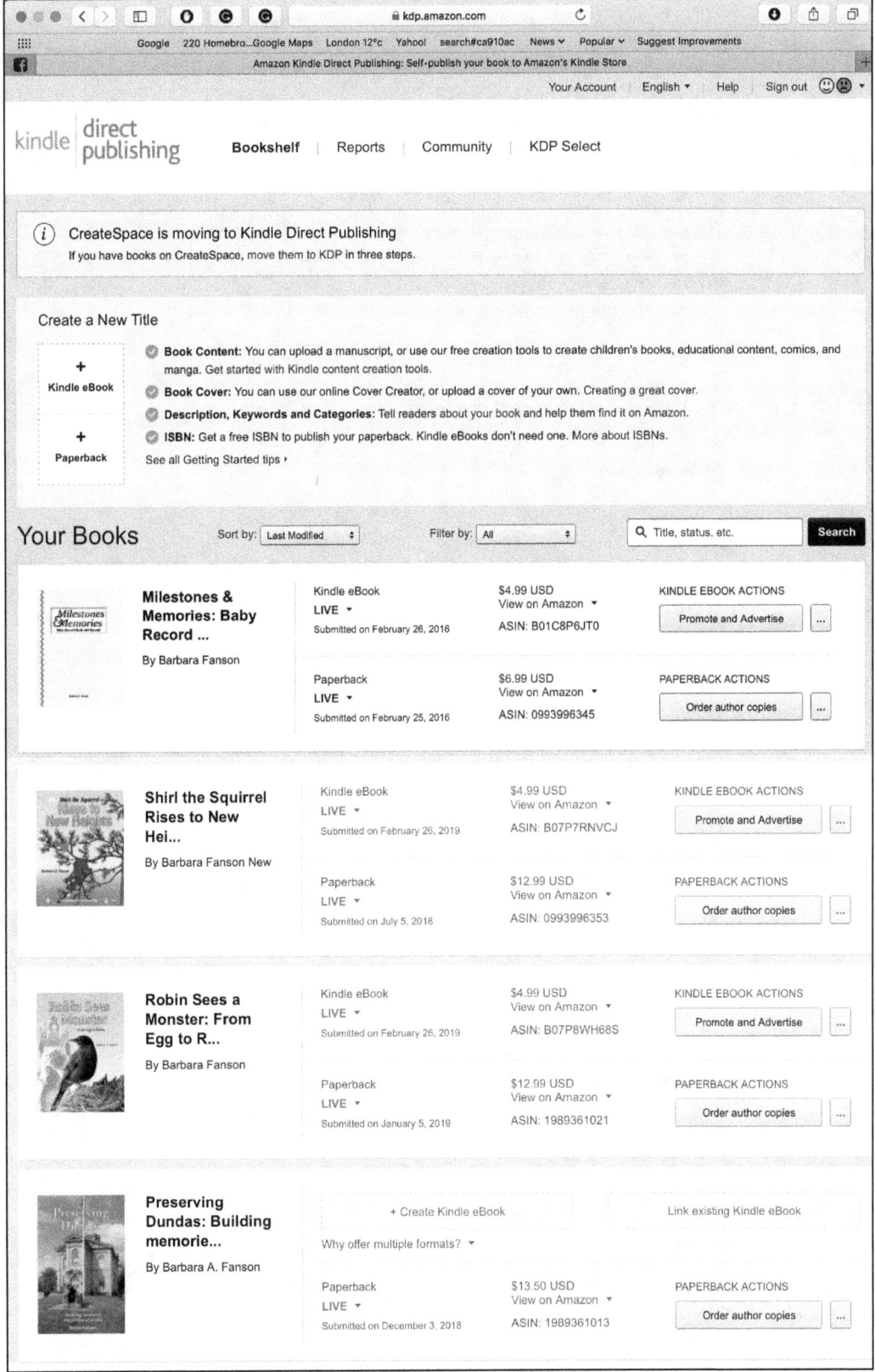

5. The next window must be completed by filling in the fields.

| Description | This will appear on your book's Amazon detail page. Why do book descriptions matter? ▼ |
|---|---|
| | Get Your Book Published focuses on producing your books—1 copy or 100 copies. Find out about Print-On-Demand printing, online uploading and publishing, and how you can sell copies worldwide. Gain valuable information on designing the interior pages of a book and how to create a book cover. Discover where to get an ISBN or barcode for the back cover. |
| | 2809 characters left |

| Publishing Rights | ● I own the copyright and I hold necessary publishing rights. What are publishing rights? ▼ |
|---|---|
| | ○ This is a public domain work What is a public domain work? ▼ |

| Keywords | Choose up to 7 keywords that describe your book. To enter the Kindle Storyteller contest, you need to add the keyword *StorytellerUK2019*. How do I choose keywords? ▼ |
|---|---|
| | **Your Keywords** (Optional) |
| | Publishing / Self-Publishing |
| | Book Publishing / Book Design |
| | Book Distribution / Book Sales |
| | Desktop Publishing |

| Categories | Choose up to two browse categories. Why are categories important? ▼ |
|---|---|
| | Nonfiction > Language Arts & Disciplines > Composition & Creative Writing |
| | Nonfiction > Design > Book |
| | [ Choose categories ] |
| | ☐ Large print. What is large print? ▼ |

| Adult Content | Does this book contain language, situations, or images inappropriate for children under 18 years of age? |
|---|---|
| | ● No |
| | ○ Yes |

[ Save as Draft ]  [ Save and Continue ]

Next step: Content

*Barbara A. Fanson*

6. If your book is going to be on a shelf in a bookstore or library, what section would it be in? You can choose up to 2 categories:
Fiction
Nonfiction
Juvenile Fiction
Juvenile Nonfiction
Comics & Graphic Novels
Education & Reference
Literary Collections
Non-Classifiable.

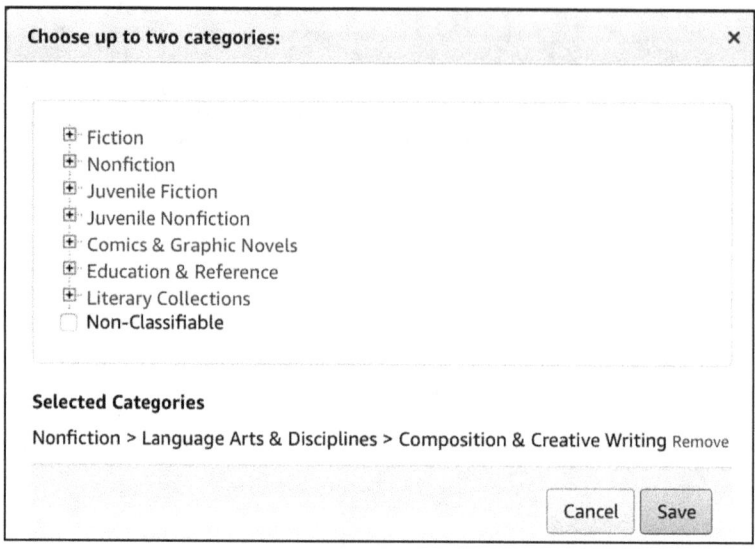

7. When choosing a category, just click on the + sign to expand the topics.
I opened Nonfiction, opened Language Arts & Disciplines, and chose Publishing.
I also opened Nonfiction, opened Language Arts & Disciplines, and chose Composition & Creative Writing.

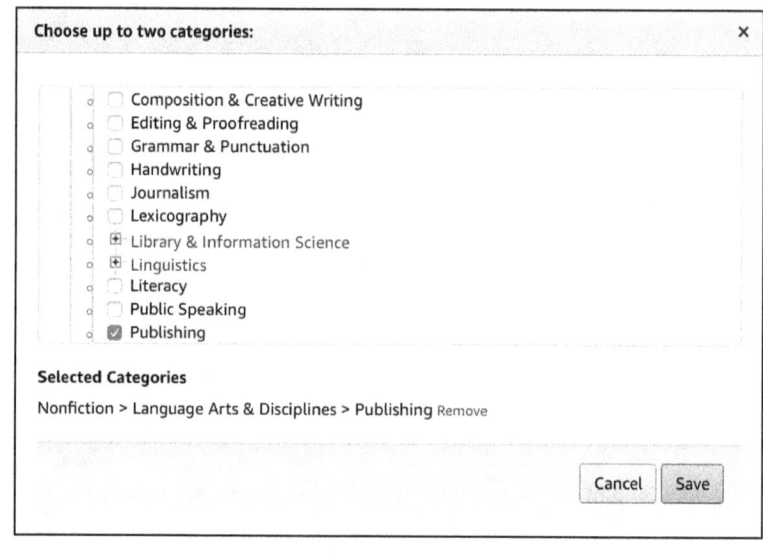

8. When you're finished with this page, click on the Save and Continue button at the bottom.

9. A new window opens to create Paperback Content.

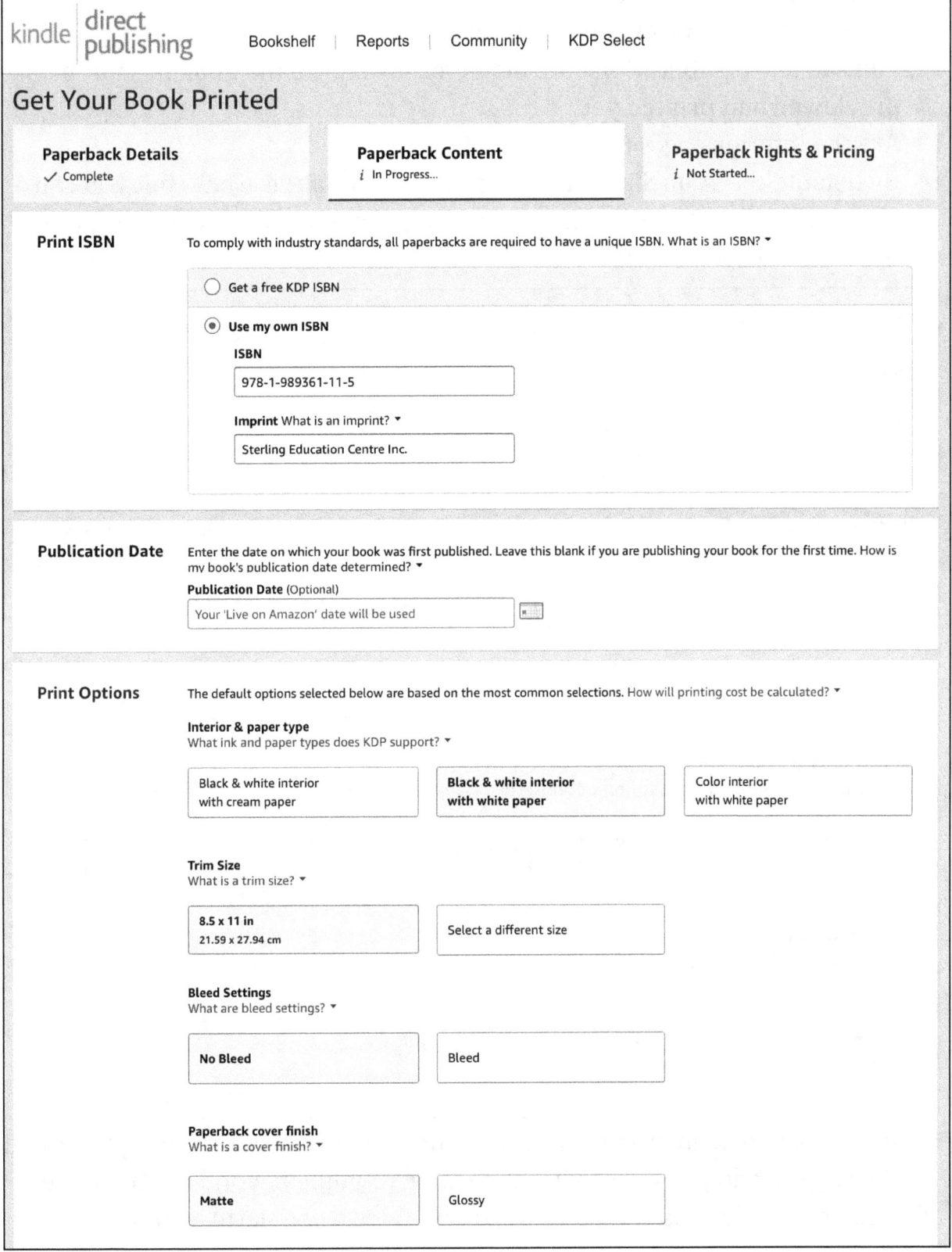

10. Do you have an ISBN (International Standard Book Number) or do you want KDP to supply one?
11. Imprint is the name of your company or your name.
12. You can leave publication date blank for now since the book has not been previewed and printed yet.
13. Are the interior pages black and white or color?
14. By default, the Trim Size (finished size of the book) is 6"x9", but you can click on the Select a Different Size button, and a window opens to choose the trim size for your book.

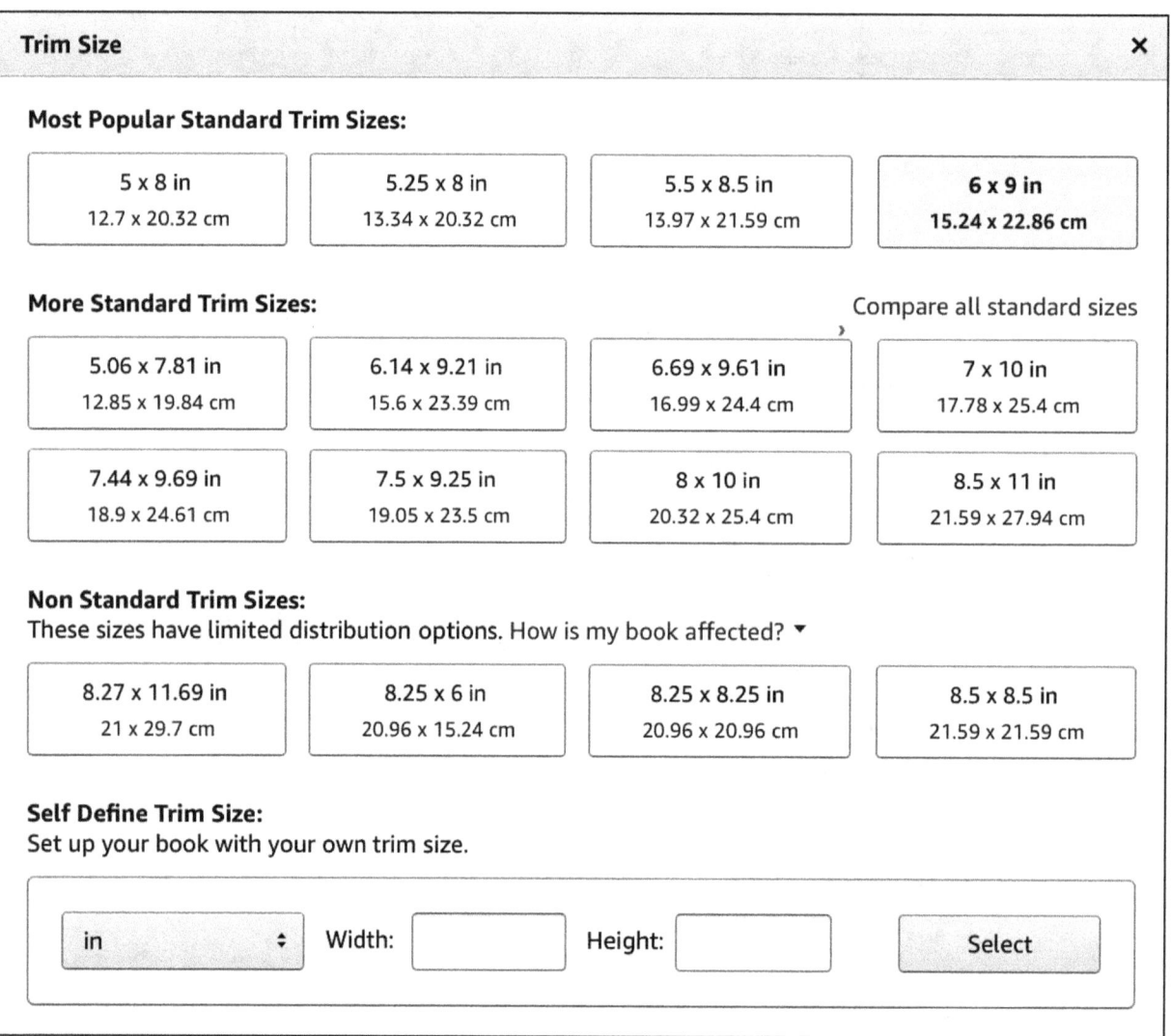

15. Does your book have a bleed? Does your book have a white margin around the edges or do you have images bleeding or going beyond the trim size?
16. What type of lamination do you want on the cover? Matte or Glossy?

17. Click on the Upload Paperback Manuscript button to upload the file for interior pages, if you're ready.

    For best results, KDP recommends a formatted PDF file, but they will accept Word Doc or Docx, HTML files, or RTF.

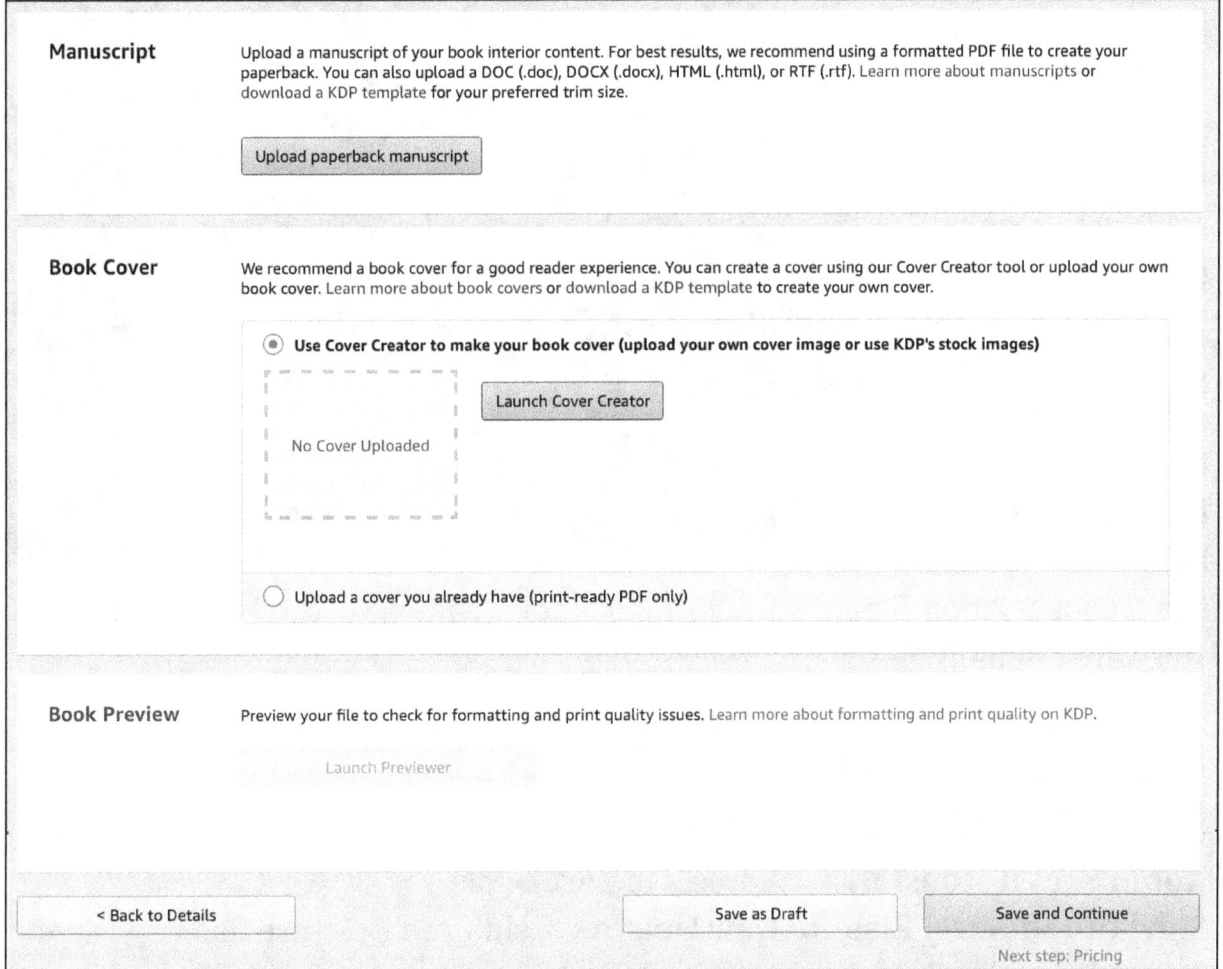

18. You can upload the print-ready Cover PDF file for your book cover or use their Cover Creator tool. Print-ready artwork uses CMYK color, 300-ppi resolution or higher, with art showing back cover, spine, and front cover.

19. After you have uploaded the interior pages and cover of your paperback manuscript, you can preview the book to check for formatting and print quality issues.

    You can click on Launch Previewer or download a PDF of the book to proof the book.

# About the Author

Barbara A. Fanson is an author, graphic designer, and retired college professor. She had 2 books published by Self-Counsel Press, a traditional book publisher, and has self-published over 30 books. She has written and illustrated 2 children's picture books, a historical fiction book, 2 non-fiction photographic books, a baby record book, and 20 software manuals.

Publishing has changed so much since she got her first computer.

She enjoys hiking and photography when not feeding squirrels. She lives in Mount Hope, Ontario with a dashing black cat, 2 Robins, 7 squirrels, a chipmunk, a rabbit, and a human family.

**Robin Sees a Monster**, a children's picture book
**Shirl the Squirrel Rises to New Heights**, a children's picture book
**Tragedy on the Twenty**, a historical fiction book
**Milestones & Memories**, a baby record book & beyond
**Preserving Dundas**, building memories one picture at a time
**Preserving Smithville**, building memories one picture at a time
**Photoshop**, one step at a time instruction book
**Start & Run a Desktop Publishing Business**, a how-to business book published by Self-Counsel Press
**Producing a First-Class Newsletter**, a how-to business book published by Self-Counsel Press.

# Book Publishing Terms

*Terminology used in Get Your Book Published*

**Advance:** Sometimes an author will paid a portion of their royalties in advance or before book sales.

**Barcode:** A series of black lines with different widths, which are readable by a machine. They often indicate the price or ISBN of a book.

**Binding:** The way pages are held together in a book: glue, stitching, or sewn.

**Bleed:** Printing that goes beyond the Trim Size of a page.

**Book:** A collection of pages bound together.

**Cataloguing in Publication (CIP) Data:** This is a voluntary program provided by the National Library of Canada in which books are catalogued before they are published. www.collectionscanada.gc.ca

**Coil Binding:** Also called spiral binding, where a metal or plastic wire is spiraled through holes punched along the side of a stack of paper. Often used for reports, proposals and manuals. Documents bound with coil have the ability to lay flat and can rotate 360 degrees.

**Comb binding:** Binding a stack of paper together by inserting the teeth of a flexible plastic comb into holes punched along one of the edges. Often used for catalogs, reports and manuals.

**CMYK:** Cyan, magenta, yellow, and black ink is used to print color materials.

**Design:** The format of the cover art and interior design (page layout, front matter, graphical elements, headers/footers, page numbers, folio information, etc.)

**Distributor:** A company who stores your books in a warehouse, prepares orders, and ships books to retail outlets.

**Dust jacket:** For an additional fee, you can have a paper wrap around your book to protect it.

**Editing:** Editors look for grammatical and spelling errors, and inconsistencies.

**EPS:** Electronic PostScript is a file format for saving images. Artwork created in Adobe Illustrator is often saved as an EPS.

**Galley:** The preliminary proofs of a manuscript. They are meant to be reviewed by authors, editors, and designers.

**GIF:** Graphic Interchange Format is a file format that is used in website design or social media.

**Imprint:** The name and address of the publisher, which appears in the front matter of a book.

**Independent Press:** Also called a micro-press, small publishing companies, which are not part of a large publishing house.

**ISBN:** International Standard Book Number. You should have an ISBN for your book so bookstores, libraries, and schools can order and catalog books. The ISBN is associated with certain information about your book, including the language in which it is published, the format in which it is published, who published it, and more. In Canada, you can get it free: www.collectionscanada.gc.ca

**Metadata:** Metadata is the key to standing out in a crowded book market. Metadata helps to get your book found. What words would people use to search for your book?

**Micro-press:** An Independent Press/Publisher who may only have produced one or two titles.

**Pay-to-Print Publishing:** Sometimes called Vanity Press, Pay-to-Print publishers offer print services, ISBN registration, and sometimes editorial and design services, but do not offer marketing or distribution services to self-published authors.

**Perfect Bind:** Books with pages glued together and attached to a cover. Usually paperback or softcover.

Pixels per inch (PPI): When images are scanned into a computer or photos taken on a digital camera, they are captured with 72 pixels per inch or 300 pixels per inch or whatever.

**PNG:** Portable Network Graphic is a file format for saving images that will be used in website design.

**Printer:** Or print shop prints the final, editing book onto paper and binds it.

**Print-on-Demand:** a process of printing individual copies or small numbers of a book using digital technology.

**Proofreading:** Proofreaders read proofs or galleys of edited manuscripts. They look for consistency of page design, page numbering, typos, and layout, etc.

**Publisher:** A publisher is a person, corporation, or group that undertakes the production of a creative work from manuscript to market-ready book. A publisher is not a printer. A publisher usually undertakes the financial responsibility of the book and sales.

**Publishing Consultants:** Small, independent presses offer publishing services (editorial services, design services, distribution and/or marketing services) for payment. This is different from Vanity Publishing in that Publishing Consultants provide services to the author but do not market to the author.

**RGB:** Red, green, and blue colors are used on color computers, televisions, and electronic devices.

**Royalty:** Royalties are payments made to authors based on the sales of their books. Publishers will sign a contract with their authors outlining what the Royalties for book sales will be. Royalties range from 5% of sales to 15% of sales. Therefore, if you have an agreement with your author to pay a 10% royalty on gross sales, and the author's book retails for $10, you will be paying your author $1 for every book sold.

**Saddle-StitchBinding:** A simple form of binding in which pages are stapled through the middle of folded pages.

**Self-Publishing:** Self-Publishers create the manuscript and then produce it themselves or hire editors, designers, and printers to finish the production. Self-Publishing has become much easier with advances in technology and desktop publishing software, however, Self-Publishers still face most of the difficulties of traditional publishers in terms of securing distribution, marketing, and promotion.

**Stitched Bind:** Books with pages stitched together and sewn to a cover, usually hardcover.

**TIF or TIFF:** Tagged Image File Format is a file format for saving photos, often used for printing materials.

**Trim Size:** The actual size of the page after it has been trimmed. Most books are not printed standard-sized paper. Books are usually printed on larger sheets of paper, folded, and then trimmed to size.

**Vanity Press:** Authors may choose to pay a Vanity Press business to print their books. Vanity Presses will produce any book, regardless of the genre

*Barbara A. Fanson*